The Economic and Social Research Institute

The Economic and Social Research Institute (ESRI) is a non-profit organisation which was founded in 1960 as The Economic Research Institute. The Institute is a private company, limited by guarantee, and enjoys full academic independence. It is governed by a Council consisting of 32 members who are representative of business, trade unions, government departments, state agencies, universities and other research institutes.

The ESRI's *General Research Series* is the primary research series of the Institute and is intended for the publication of the findings of a substantial research project. It is concerned mainly with research undertaken by the author on topics which lend themselves to the use of more scientific and technical methods of analysis. The conclusions drawn in the paper tend to be confined to those that stem directly from the author's own research findings. Papers published in the series are subject to a rigorous refereeing procedure. The first draft of the paper is read by two staff members, who evaluate the paper as a whole. The revised version is then sent for comment to organisations with a more direct interest in the subject matter, such as government departments, trade unions, employers' organisations, state agencies, etc. The paper may be revised in the light of their comments. The revised draft is then sent to an external referee known only to the Director of the Institute, at an academic institution in Ireland or abroad. The recommendation of this referee in regard to publication is normally decisive, though the final responsibility for deciding whether and in what form all work undertaken at the ESRI is published rests solely with the Director.

TRADING QUALIFICATIONS FOR JOBS

Overeducation and the Irish Youth Labour Market

D. F. Hannan
B. McCabe
and
S. McCoy

Oak Tree Press
Dublin
In association with
The Economic and Social Research Institute

Oak Tree Press
Merrion Building
Lower Merrion Street
Dublin 2, Ireland
http://www.oaktreepress.com

A catalogue record of this book is
available from the British Library.

ISBN 1-86076-106-2

Printed in Ireland by Colour Books Ltd.

Contents

List of Tables and Figures

Table

Figure

Acknowledgements

We owe a special debt of gratitude to the Department of Education, who funded the main costs incurred in undertaking this project. We are especially grateful for the untiring support of Oliver Cussen, former Assistant Secretary at the Department; his incisive critiques of earlier drafts were very helpful.

Within The Economic and Social Research Institute, the book owes much to the critical comments and suggestions of the two internal referees, Chris Whelan and Brian Nolan. Mary Cleary and the General Office staff have been most efficient in preparing the various drafts. We would also like to express our appreciation to Deirdre Whitaker for careful editing of the document.

The contribution of Brian Langan of Oak Tree Press, in carefully editing the final document, is also appreciated. In addition, we would like to note the helpful comments and critiques of personnel in the Departments of Enterprise and Employment and Finance. Finally, we are grateful for the helpful comments from the anonymous external referee.

Any remaining errors or omissions are the sole responsibility of the authors.

About the Authors

Damian F. Hannan, PhD, MRIA, is a Research Professor at The Economic and Social Research Institute. He was formerly Professor of Social Theory and Institutions at University College Cork.

Breda McCabe, M. Soc. Sc., is a former Research Assistant at The Economic and Social Research Institute. She is currently a doctoral student at the University of Toronto.

Selina McCoy, M. Soc. Sc., is an Assistant Research Officer at The Economic and Social Research Institute. She is also currently completing her doctorate at The Queen's University of Belfast.

Chapter 1

The Relationship between Educational and Occupational Achievement in the Irish Youth Labour Market

INTRODUCTION

The main research question addressed in this study is whether a high degree of overlap exists in the status of occupations taken up by second level school-leavers and third level graduates — particularly the extent and nature of "overqualification" amongst third level graduates. Stated more formally, the question becomes: What is the extent and nature of congruence between level of education attained and level of occupational status subsequently achieved in the Irish youth labour market? Does an increasing level of education pay off in higher occupational attainment, or is there a high degree of overlap or correspondence in the type and level of occupations taken up by those with different levels of education? State policy assumes a low degree of overlap, or a high rate of return to third level education — given its substantially greater cost. But is this the case? This study sets out to answer this question.

The rapid growth of third level educational participation in Ireland since the late 1970s appears at times to have significantly outstripped the expansion of occupational opportunities at an equivalent status level — i.e., those previously characteristic of third level entrants. So, critiques of our rapid third level expansion policy have focused on the extent to which third level graduates take up jobs previously taken up by those with a Leaving Certificate, as well as the latter group's take-up of jobs previously "reserved" for those with junior cycle or lower qualifications. Earlier work by Breen (1984a) and Hannan (1986) showed a substantial growth in "qualification inflation" for those entering the labour market with second level qualifications at the beginning of the 1980s; with a variant of the American "diploma disease" (Dore, 1976) apparently characterising Irish educational and employment experience at that time. Later results up to 1992 (Hannan and Smyth, 1994) showed a continuation of that pattern. One serious result was that those with poor or no qualifications were being pushed so far down the labour queue that they became disproportionately unemployed (Hannan, 1996; NESF, 1997).

There is a widespread presumption of a high degree of vertical, stratified matching — or "level congruence" (Allmendinger, 1989) — of jobs/occupations and educational levels in the Irish labour market, with Junior Certificate entrants, for instance, taking up unskilled or semi-skilled manual and service occupations, while at the other extreme, university graduates enter the higher reaches of the occupational/professional hierarchy. While there is strong evidence of high returns to increasing levels of education in terms of employment, income and occupational status in the Irish labour market (Breen *et al.*, 1995; Callan *et al.*, 1993, 1997; Smyth and Surridge, 1996), as well as significant differences in the distribution of educational levels by occupational category (Sexton *et al.*, 1996), very little research work has been done on the extent of such stratified "matching" of different educational levels with occupational status levels amongst new job entrants. The extent to which entry to the Irish labour market is non-competitive between levels of education, or the extent to which there is high "level congruence" in Irish education/labour-market linkages, is the main question explored in this research (Allmendinger, 1989; Hannan *et al.*, 1996).

Main Research Questions

We attempt to answer five basic research questions in this study:

1. *What is the extent and nature of the congruence/correlation between school/college leavers' level of education and the occupational status of first job achieved?* The higher the degree of "level congruence", or the lower the degree of "overlap", between educational level and the occupational status of first jobs achieved, the lower the problem of "overqualification".

2. *To what extent, however, do first jobs — even if we exclude casual and temporary part-time jobs — provide a reasonable estimate of the medium-*

term occupational status achievements of upper second level and third level school/college leavers? Some evidence from abroad suggests that, although there may well be substantial initial "occupational overlaps" between levels of education, greater upward career mobility occurs amongst those with higher (third level) qualifications entering the labour market — particularly those taking up "second level jobs". As a result "overeducation" is merely a temporary phenomenon. To what extent does this hold for Ireland?

3. *What role does migration — both internal and international (emigration) — play in "successful" labour market integration for different levels of education?* From previous work (NESC, 1991), it is clear that successful emigration is selective of the more upwardly mobile second and third level leavers; and that local and national labour markets are differently structured by educational level and occupational status. Outside the larger cities, local labour markets appear to be more informally structured, catering disproportionately for those with lower- to middle-level qualifications entering equivalent levels of the labour market. The national labour market (with Dublin at its apex) is generally structured more formally — with more formal methods of recruitment, using more objective, universalistic criteria, and catering for a generally higher (lower non-manual to professional) level of occupational recruitment. Successful integration into the international labour market is even more dependent on high levels of qualification.

4. *Where third level graduates are "overqualified" for their occupations, to what extent are they rewarded (in higher wages/salaries, for instance) for their better qualifications or greater human capital?* Most of the research literature suggests they are: with the substantial variation in job characteristics and associated job rewards found within any occupational category being highly associated with a worker's level of education or human capital characteristics.

5. *Where third level graduates initially take up lower status, or "second level" jobs, to what extent are their subsequent career mobility chances affected by such employment, particularly if they first enter the "secondary sector" of the labour market?* Taking a labour market segmentation approach, it is clear that young workers are disproportionately concentrated in "secondary sectors" of the economy — primarily in

less skilled jobs in non-goods-producing industries. These demand-side characteristics of the youth labour market are dealt with separately in Chapter 6, as are the consequences of "secondary sector" location for earnings and career mobility.

To provide answers to these questions, we analyse extensive educational and labour market data from a follow-up survey of (second level) school leavers. The national survey is of school leavers who left in the school year 1985/86 and were first interviewed in mid-1987, and re-interviewed in late 1992: one and six years after they completed their second level education. The initial 1987 survey, although carried out in a period of very stringent government cutbacks, nevertheless occurs at a point where the worst of the recession was over (see Smyth and Surridge, 1995 and 1996, for a review of youth employment trends over the 1980s), with significant employment growth up to 1991.

In the following sections, we first provide a short review of the underlying theoretical orientations that guide research in this area; and second, we review research evidence on the "overqualification" debate — one that has a large and contentious literature since at least the mid-1970s (Dore, *The Diploma Disease*, 1976). We conclude with a small number of guiding hypotheses, which will then structure the analyses. We start, however, with a brief description of the main features of the Irish education system, as well as the nature of the linkages between what it is that the educational system produces — school and college leavers with various levels and types of educational qualifications — and what it is that employers appear to value in their employment decisions.

The Irish Educational System in Comparative Perspective

Three main institutional features of the educational system and their relationships to labour market entry processes are normally emphasised: their degree of differentiation and associated stratification; their degree of standardisation; and the nature and strength of the linkage between the educational and labour market system (Hannan *et al.*, 1996; Shavit and Müller, 1998).

Standardisation refers to the extent to which curricula and examinations are state-regulated and nationally standardised. In this sense, the Irish full-time second-level system is one of the most state-regulated and centralised in the OECD. As a result, level of education reached and examination grades achieved can be taken as equally valid and highly reliable, irrespective of school attended or region of origin — a situation that does not hold equally in many OECD countries, most notably the United States (Shavit and Müller, 1998; Hannan *et al.*, 1996). Perhaps partly as a result, employers appear to pay more attention to such educational qualification in the Irish case than in others (see Breen *et al.*, 1995).

The Irish second level educational system, however, is not highly differentiated into separate curricular tracks with separate examinations. At lower second level, it is relatively undifferentiated and generally comprehensive in curricular and examination terms. There is now greater differentiation at upper second level, as the percentage of the youth cohort staying on goes over 80 per cent. The new Leaving Certificate Vocational Programme (LCVP) and Leaving Certificate Applied Programme (LCAP) were specifically developed for those whose aptitudes and orientations were not adequately catered for by the conventional more academic programme. However, for the sample interviewed in this survey (1985/86), both the lower and upper second level was effectively undifferentiated. Compared to German, Dutch or even British provision for upper second level education, the Irish system is still very homogeneous (Shavit and Müller, 1998). Perhaps partly because it is so undifferentiated and so standardised, our educational qualifications appear to be highly stratified: the higher the level of qualification and the higher the examination grades, the more valuable the qualification (Breen *et al.*, 1995).

Finally, there is little direct institutionalised linkage between the educational system and its outputs and the employment system and its intakes. Unlike the German "dual system", for instance, there is an extremely low level of apprenticeship training in Ireland. While around half of the annual intake into the labour market in Germany is through three- to four-year apprenticeships, the figure here is now less than ten per cent and at the time of the survey was not much more than five per cent. There are, therefore, only a very limited range of occupational "entry points" — mainly in skilled manual, craft and professional/technical occupations — which require occupationally specific education and training. Effectively, therefore, for the great majority of school leavers entering the Irish labour market, employers are free to choose amongst job applicants on the basis of criteria they set for themselves. Given the high degree of standardisation and effective unidimensional stratification of Irish educational qualifications, employers appear to pay proportionally greater attention to level of education and examination grades — i.e., the measures of general human capital — than is true of most of the OECD countries (Breen *et al.*, 1995).

RESEARCH REVIEW

Relevant Theoretical Orientations

We can broadly divide the relevant theoretical orientations that guide research work in this area into two: "human capital" and "screening" or "sorting and queuing" theories. Classic human capital theory (Schultz, 1961; Becker, 1964; and Freeman, 1976) basically emphasises the match between the content of what it is that is manifestly taught, or latently acquired, through formal and informal socialisation in schools/colleges and what it is that is subsequently required/used in the labour market. Essentially, this view holds that education increases the usable knowledge, skills, work habits and improves the relevant attitudes/aptitudes of students and potential workers. It consequently increases their potential labour productivity, and also decreases their subsequent training costs to employers. It is, therefore, the content of the cognitive, affective, normative and behavioural changes brought about directly or indirectly through both the formal instructional/curricular arrangements of schools, as well as through the informal social life of the school, that accounts for the increased productivity of potential workers. This enhanced "human capital" will then be expressed in the consequent differences in employment chances, occupational/career quality, and wages and wage growth associated with higher levels and quality of education. More recent formulations of the theory include some of the original "social capital" critiques of the original raw theory (Becker, 1964). Authors like Bowles and Gintis (1976) emphasised the highly class-structured nature of educational socialisation, emphasising the social reproduction functions of education in training young, working class pupils to accept their position in economic and social life — by essentially socialising them to their expected roles in the economy and society. These socialisation effects were as much indirect — in lower self-images, ability to take orders, readiness to be disciplined etc. — as direct, through lower educational expectations and achievements. Leaving the "social reproduction" thesis aside, however, the indirect, latent socialisation effects of successful schooling in developing traits and competencies — such as perseverance on tasks, timekeeping, competitiveness, ability to follow orders — are of significant benefit to employers if they are adequately measured or indexed, even indirectly, by educational certifications.

At its extreme, the set of sorting/screening and signalling theories (Arrow, 1973; Spence, 1973), on the other hand, emphasise the assessment/certification role of schools in publicly validating the underlying abilities and aptitudes of school leavers, not the content of what had been learned in school, or even the personal qualities developed or improved there. Such certifications provide signals to potential employers of the innate ability/aptitude levels of pupils (and, therefore, their potential productivity levels as workers) — individual attributes which schools are very good at measuring (Stiglitz, 1975). At its most extreme, the curricular content and level of what it is that pupils learn at school (and are certified as having learned) is, therefore, less important in this framework than the latent function that schools serve in sorting pupils according to their innate abilities, learning potential and potential labour productivity levels. Employers can thus select those that will be most suitable and least costly to train.

It has proved extremely difficult to separate out the relative effects of the educationally substantive function and the signalling/screening (of underlying abilities and aptitudes) function of educational qualifications on initial employment decisions, or on subsequent work histories, etc. This research is no different in that respect. Our research design does not allow us to test the relative validity of either set of "theories". We assume, however, that both are present: that employers make decisions both on the basis of what standardised credentials tell them about what curriculum school leavers have learned and how well they have done so; as well as providing important information about the relative "underlying ability" levels of school leavers, their relative expectations/attitudes and work-related aptitudes. Our measures are limited to "level of education" achieved, as well as level of performance in examinations.

The Meaning and Extent of Overeducation

Variously referred to as underutilisation, qualification inflation, overqualification, credentialism, surplus education, and so on, "overeducation" can be broadly defined in objective terms as:

> . . . the incongruity between a person's level of education and the level of education typical of that person's occupation (Smith, 1986).

In the Irish case, the concept, though not the term, has mainly been used to refer to the extent to which ever-higher levels of education were being required for lower to middle status occupations from the early 1980s onwards.

Breen's (1984a) and Hannan's (1986) work showed clearly that, as unemployment grew in the early 1980s — and specifically with the rapid decline in non-manual jobs as governments cut back on public service employment — there was a rapid growth in the extent to which those with a Leaving Certificate took up unskilled and semi-skilled manual and service jobs, employment which previously had been monopolised by those with lower level qualifications or none. As it appears very unlikely that the nature and "difficulty" of such semi-skilled and unskilled manual and service jobs could have become upgraded at such a fast pace between 1979 and 1983, it appeared much more reasonable to assume that, as labour queues grew, employers increasingly "picked off the top" on the basis of the level of educational qualifications of job applicants. This trend toward an increasing appropriation of lower manual and service jobs by those with a Leaving Certificate qualification increased significantly over the 1980s — as youth unemployment remained very high and the percentage of the cohort going on to complete the Leaving Certificate course increased rapidly (Sexton *et al.*, 1996; Hannan and Smyth, 1995; Smyth and Surridge, 1996).

Estimates of the extent to which third level graduates are taking up second level jobs are limited in Ireland, but findings from the United States and Canada are enlightening. Hecker (1992) estimated that, in the US in 1990, 20 per cent of all workers with college degrees were either unemployed or employed in jobs requiring only high school diplomas. In 1970, the figure was 11 per cent. On these grounds, Hecker concludes that the American economy is generating college graduates faster than it is generating jobs for those graduates. Equally, Hunter (1988), in examining the relationship between formal education and occupational allocation between 1930 and 1980 in Canada, concluded that both the importance of formal education in allocating persons to jobs at different levels of skills had increased, but that "overqualification" had also increased, particularly in the later period. However, these findings have subsequently been disputed by Tyler *et al.* (1995), who argue that Hecker's conclusions stem from his decision to focus on a highly aggregate statistic: the 1970–90 change in the proportion of all college graduates holding "high school jobs". They argue for the need to examine in more detail recent changes in the labour market for young people. In particular, they demonstrate that, while a small but growing proportion of college graduates took jobs requiring second level education in the 1980s, it was mainly older men who bore the brunt of white collar restructuring. Furthermore, the skill requirements of many occupations had risen, with many occupations previously requiring only second level education now requiring college education. Essentially, Tyler *et al.* point to the need to examine the recent experiences of young labour market entrants separately, given the changing skill requirements of some jobs, along with structural changes in the economy. And in their own study, they show that over the late 1980s to early 1990s the extent of overeducation had not increased, while the returns to college education had in fact increased considerably.

In the Irish context, there is some evidence of an increase in overeducation and growing credentialism. Work carried out by Hannan and Smyth (1995) suggests that jobs that were previously occupied by those who left school either at or before the Junior Cycle level are increasingly being filled by those with Leaving Certificate and higher qualifications. To illustrate: the bulk of entrants to skilled and semi-skilled manual jobs in 1980 left school prior to the Leaving Certificate; by 1992, the majority had secured at least the Leaving Certificate. Pre-Leaving Certificate school leavers represented 72 per cent of male, skilled and semi-skilled manual workers in 1980, but only 40 per cent by 1992. While the nature of the work demanded by these jobs may well have changed over the period, it appears likely that most Leaving Certificate and third level graduates occupying skilled and semi-skilled manual jobs in 1992 were "overqualified" for these jobs.

"Overqualification": a Temporary or Permanent State?

The initial period of transition and adjustment in the labour market amongst young, recently qualified workers frequently includes a period of job search or job shopping/swapping (Cregan, 1991), characterised by frequent job changes which are both employee- and employer-initiated. So, for a substantial proportion of young people, it may take some time before they secure employment commensurate with their qualifications. According to this kind of "matching" argument (Johnson, 1978; Jovanovic, 1979; Viscusi, 1980), over-education is a temporary condition for a significant proportion of workers. Interestingly, there appear to be important gender differences in such job search behaviour. While no significant gender differences occur in the frequency of job separation and job-swapping, substantial gender differences occur in the financial pay-offs to such job-swapping. On average, job-swapping by males in the United States paid off financially, while frequently it did not for females. Male, working class early school leavers in particular appeared to confront a range of jobs with a greater range of financial rewards than that encountered by females (Cregan, 1991). This relates to Dex's (1982) socialisation hypothesis that female job search behaviour might be motivated to a greater extent by psychic or social status rewards (e.g. a more "appropriate" occupation) rather than financial/material rewards.

If there is some substance to the "job shopping" hypothesis, we would expect that the "overeducated" would more frequently change jobs and also be more likely to be upwardly mobile over time in the labour market. Sicherman (1991) did find that "overeducated" workers were more likely to change firms, change occupations and move to higher-ranked occupations within the following year than those appropriately educated for their work. However, not all studies support this conclusion. Robst (1995), for instance, suggests that Sicherman's (1991) findings of greater mobility for overeducated workers may be attributed to greater average mobility in jobs that require less schooling.

Extent to which the Overeducated are Rewarded for their Better Qualifications

Where college/university graduates take up occupations mainly composed of workers with second level education (i.e., "second level jobs"), they may still get better jobs within that occupational category — in terms of "job difficulty", complexity, degree of autonomy and responsibility, etc. — and be rewarded for this. As Tyler *et al.* (1995) point out, there is a need for greater detail on "high school jobs" before one can conclude that "overeducated workers" are disadvantaged relative to their similarly qualified counterparts who are occupationally/educationally matched; or that overeducated workers are no better off than those in the same occupations who are more "appropriately matched" to their jobs. Their findings show that, while college graduates in "high school jobs" have lower earnings than other college "level congruent" graduates, they still earn more than second level graduates in similar jobs; i.e., even within occupations, the higher the level of education, the greater the wage/salary levels. These results are supported by many other studies (Duncan and Hoffman, 1981; Hartog and Oosterbeek, 1988; Sichermann, 1991). Shockey's 1989 study essentially supports this conclusion, and he concludes that the primary impact of advanced education among occupationally mismatched workers is through the attainment of jobs, within occupational categories, which offer higher pay rather than high "matched (occupational) status"; whereas, amongst matched workers, the main influence of schooling is occupationally direct rather than through individually variable job characteristics within occupational categories.[1]

---

[1] There are some significant differences amongst researchers in how they measure "overeducation". Some, like Sicherman (1991), measure it in terms of respondents' perceptions of "how much formal education is required" to get or effectively carry out the job. Others, like Tyler *et al.,* (1995), use objective statistical measures — like our standard deviation below the average educational level of an occupation, etc. Some of the varying results may then be due to the varying measures.

Promotion Chances

The literature suggests a number of ways in which educational qualifications might affect promotions: the first in a direct manner, the remaining two indirectly.

Evident in human capital and status attainment work, and also in radical (Bowles and Gintis, 1976) and cultural capital interpretations, schooling (through direct instruction/learning) can be viewed as directly enhancing the cognitive, affective, normative and interpersonal knowledge, skills and aptitudes of individuals in ways that make them more productive. In addition, the indirect socialisation effects of schooling, in building up relevant aptitudes and competencies, can be as important as the direct instructional effects. In this perspective, more highly educated workers are considered more promotable because their schooling has made them both more productive and more "trainable", or less costly to train (Wilensky and Lawrence, 1979). Essentially, schooling is viewed as providing the general background knowledge, skills and dispositions needed to master the more specific skills of the workplace — hence, the more highly educated are more promotable. However, it may well be that more highly educated workers are promoted more because they are more likely to get jobs in firms with career or "job ladders" — not so much because employers are directly rewarding more educated/productive workers, but because higher level certificates/qualifications provide access to larger and more complex firms that provide such opportunities (Thurow, 1975).

Regarding the differential experiences of "overeducated", "undereducated" and "matched" workers, while much of the job-matching literature argues that the rate of job movement is greatest where the fit between individual educational/training resources and job requirements is poor, research results indicate a more complex mobility process (Spilerman and Lunde, 1991). This study indicates that the rate of (internal) promotion is maximised when the fit between education and job requirements is best, but inter-firm mobility is more likely when the fit is poor. Where an employee terminates employment and moves to another job, "promotion" is through firm/job mobility. Internal promotion, on the other hand, is decided by the employer, based on the worker's productivity. Hence, those who most closely meet the requirements of the job are most likely to be internally promoted; while, as previously indicated, mobility to new employment is most frequent amongst those with surplus education. In this context, they conclude, it is preferable to enter an organisation at a rank in which one's educational attainment is not much below the norm for the grade because, once appointed, superior ("surplus") education provides little return in internal promotion prospects.

Similar results emerged from case studies of six Chicago organisations (incorporating 35 outside hires and 33 promotions) by Bills (1988b). All three indicators of educational achievement used were ranked higher by managers who hired externally than by managers who promoted internally. Bills concludes that, while educational credentials enhance careers by getting people through organisational gates and onto organisational ladders, once inside an organisation, credentials are of less direct value and tend to give way to indicators that employers can directly observe.

A reasonable conclusion from this literature to the Irish case would be that: (a) while the initially overeducated may be more job/ firm mobile, (b) internal promotion would appear to be more likely amongst those who are initially educationally/occupationally "matched" and working in larger firms.

Effects of Qualifications versus Years of Schooling

Do diplomas and degrees yield returns net of years of schooling? Research work in North America comparing the returns to years of schooling and educational qualifications largely point in one direction. Numerous studies have clearly demonstrated that those who have achieved third level qualifications (diplomas and degrees) secure higher status jobs and earn more, independently of the number of years of schooling they have. Hunter (1993), for example, found that while people with more years of schooling earn more, those with diplomas/degrees earn more, independent of how many years of schooling they have. Similarly, Spilerman and Lunde's (1991) work indicated that degrees have an effect, net of years of schooling. However, evidence for credentialism was modest in their study: employers reward schooling only to the extent that it is relevant to job performance. They found the particular educational features that predict advancement vary with occupational and salary grade and other job characteristics, and concluded that scholastic attainment is not compensated indiscriminately. An earlier study by Ashenfelter and Mooney (1968) came to similar conclusions. Variables such as profession, degree level and field of graduate study explained more of the variance in earnings than years of graduate study (see also Callan and Harmon, 1997).

In the American educational system, of course, where most of these studies have been carried out, the second level system is not standardised, whereas the third level is to a far greater extent (Allmendinger, 1989; Hannan *et al.*, 1996). As a result, one would not expect returns to education qualifications independent of years of schooling for second level graduates in the United States. Such are the results of Rosenbaum and Kariya's (1991) study comparing the US with Japan, Allmendinger's (1989) study comparing the US to German "dual system" countries, and Kerckhoff's (1993) study comparing the United States to countries like Britain and Ireland with highly (state) standardised second level systems. In the Irish case, therefore, we expect little if any return to years of schooling, independent of qualifications.

Overqualification by Occupational Status and Educational Level

The extent to which an "occupational labour market" exists in a country — such that both "level" and "type" of education/training are institutionally required for job entry, as in the German "dual system", or in apprenticeships and professionalised occupations in most European countries — is bound to have a substantial impact on both "level congruence" and "content congruence" (Allmendinger, 1989). There is a much higher rate of "level" and "content congruence" in the German "dual system" countries, as well as in countries with highly occupationalised labour markets, like the Netherlands (see Allmendinger, 1989; Müller *et al.*, 1996; Hannan *et al.*, 1996).

Besides such "occupationalised" education and training prerequisites, there are likely to be substantial variations in the demand for graduates of different subjects/disciplines, with graduates in some areas having skills that are in surplus, and having to take whatever jobs are available. Hence, it seems likely that the prevalence of overeducation is likely to vary according to educational level, field of study and subsequent employment/occupation type. In terms of occupation type, Duncan and Hoffman (1981), again in the US, found surplus education to be least common amongst professionals, managers and clerical workers; and by educational level, least common amongst those successfully graduating from college/university or high school. Overeducation was most prevalent among those with some college education and those with advanced degrees. Given the limited occupational labour market in the Irish economy — limited to those occupations with apprenticeship and professional education/training prerequisites — both "level" and "content congruence" rates are likely to be much closer to the American than the German model (Allmendinger, 1989) or even to the British system, with their much higher rates of apprenticeship training (OECD, 1996a).

In the Irish case, therefore, we expect higher levels of education/occupation "matching" (and lower "overqualification" levels) amongst skilled manual and craft occupations or other occupations requiring considerable vocational training. Overqualification is also less likely amongst those with vocational/technical or professional educational qualifications — and more likely to occur amongst those with more general and less academic qualifications (see Hannan and Ó Riain, 1993).

Community/Regional College Graduates versus University Graduates

To date, little research has been undertaken in Ireland into the relative experiences of university and regional college graduates. Drawing on work predominantly from the United States and Canada, two theoretical viewpoints emerge on the nature of the community college function (the rough equivalent of regional technical colleges with two- or three-year non-degree programmes). First, the older functionalist perspective argues that community colleges provide additional opportunities for educational/social mobility for the lower middle class and working class, as well as teaching the intermediate technical skills needed for a complex industrial/service economy. Human capital theories take much the same approach. The alternative class-reproduction perspective (as in

Bowles and Gintis, 1976; Karabel, 1972), views the community college as another element in the class-based educational tracking system, reproducing the class structure by sorting and sifting young people into educational institutions and subsequent job levels, where job status and income are closely related to type of education received and class background of students.

In a comprehensive review of previous studies on the subject, Dougherty (1987) distinguishes not only between community college graduates and their university counterparts, but also among those who aspire to a bachelor degree (or higher), an associate degree and those who seek vocational training. Results indicate that these three community college sub-groups have substantially different educational/labour market experiences and outcomes relative to their university counterparts. Degree aspirants who enter community colleges attain significantly fewer bachelor degrees and years of education than similar students who enter four-year universities. However, the converse is true of vocational aspirants: such students do significantly better if they enter a community college rather than a university or a post-secondary vocational school. To illustrate, a study by Velez (1985) of students seven years after entering college showed 79 per cent of entrants to academic programmes in universities had received a bachelor degree, compared with only 31 per cent of entrants to academic programmes in community colleges. Controlling for pre-matriculation differences in student composition and preceding achievement, the difference was reduced to 19 percentage points.

As to the occupational outcomes of graduating from both institutions, one ten-year follow-up study by Anisef *et al.* (1992) indicated that both the earnings and occupational status achieved differed substantially between the two college types. The gap in average occupational status points *increased* with length of time in the labour market. Hence, the relative disadvantage experienced by community college graduates does not diminish with time in the labour market; rather, the reverse occurred.

The earlier work of Monk-Turner (1988) and Breneman and Nelson (1981), amongst others, also concluded that community college graduates, relative to their university counterparts, were substantially disadvantaged in terms of occupational status and income received.

Bills (1988a) identified three possible reasons for the relative disadvantage of community college *academic* aspirants in the United States. In the first two years of college, a higher dropout rate occurs among community college entrants than among comparable university entrants — partly accounted for by the lower academic selectivity and other academic deficiencies of community colleges. Second, among those surviving the first two years of college, community college entrants encountered greater institutional obstacles to continuation into the upper division of universities — with many universities restricting entry from community colleges because of their greater vocational orientation. Third, even among those who enter the upper division of universities, community college entrants encounter greater institutional difficulty in securing financial aid and in becoming socially integrated, besides having poorer academic preparation for upper-division work.

A number of conclusions from this research appear reasonably justified in the Irish case. University graduates, on average, are likely to be at a significant labour market advantage over RTC certificate and diploma graduates, and that relative advantage is likely to increase over time in the labour market. Similarly, the average RTC certificate/diploma graduate is likely to be equally advantaged over those with a Leaving Certificate, etc. (see Breen *et al.*, 1995; Callan *et al.*, 1993, 1997), and recent work by Barrett and his colleagues (1997) indicates that the advantage to third level graduates appears to have significantly increased over recent times in the Irish labour market.

MAIN HYPOTHESES

The following hypotheses are proposed to guide the analysis, as inferred from the research literature reviewed:

1. The higher the level of education, the greater the employment chances, and the lower the level of education the higher the unemployment and withdrawal rate from the labour market.

2. Although there is expected to be a high degree of "level congruence" between educational output and labour market intake in Ireland, the significant degree of over-supply in the Irish labour market, particularly of those with a Leaving Certificate and higher qualifications, means that:

a) There is a high degree of occupational "overlap" between those with a Leaving Certificate qualification and those with the next lower level of qualification;

b) There is also a high degree of overlap between the former and those with a two-year, third level certificate qualification; particularly between those with post-Leaving Certificate courses and those with certificate qualifications;

c) The overlap between those with university degrees and others is expected to be low, primarily because of the high degree of institutionalisation and greater marketability of university degree qualifications.

3. "Overqualified" workers are expected to have significantly higher levels of job/firm mobility and, in current jobs, to have significantly lower levels of job satisfaction.

4. Earnings, however, are expected to be higher amongst the "overqualified" than the "matched" within the same occupational category.

5. The higher the degree of professionalisation, technical/scientific knowledge, skills or apprenticeships required for particular occupations, the greater the degree of "content" and "level congruence" between educational outputs and labour market entrants. Hence, "overqualification" is least likely and job-matching most likely to occur in professional and semi-professional occupations, occupations with pronounced technical or scientific contents, as well as in skilled manual (craft) and lower technical qualifications; i.e., in work contexts/situations that are highly "occupationalised". It is most likely to occur amongst lower status manual and service occupations, and in lower non-manual and administrative occupations.

6. Besides level of education, the type of education or field of study is also hypothesised to be important: with those taking vocational/technical specialities at second level or professional courses at third level being less likely to take/get jobs for which they are "overqualified".

7. "Overqualification" is most characteristic of first years in the labour force — at job search and first job phases, particularly

amongst third level leavers. With increased "settling down" in the labour market, "overqualified" workers are more likely to be upwardly mobile than their working colleagues who are "educationally matched" to their jobs. Over time, therefore, the rate of "overqualification" will decline significantly; with the extent of "level congruence" between educational level and jobs increasing with time in the work force.

8. We hypothesise, however, that there will be severe negative career effects for the better educated of initially taking up such low status jobs, for which they are clearly overqualified. Besides the expected negative career effect of initial lower occupational status, we also expect an additional negative interaction effect from initial "overqualification": that such labour market entrants pay an additional price for taking up such disproportionately low status occupations.

Chapter 2

Research Methods

We describe four main aspects of the research in this chapter: the methods and data sources used and the results of sampling and interviewing; some of the main characteristics of respondents; the variables and measures used to tap our main concepts; and the data analysis approach taken.

Samples and Interviews

This report is mainly based on analyses of a follow-up survey of 1985/86 school leavers, carried out in late 1992. Almost 66,000 school leavers are estimated to have left second level schools — or completed their second level education — in the academic year 1985/86. Of these, a sample of 2,090 were first interviewed in May 1987 — over 90 per cent of a fully representative, stratified, random sample of all 1985/86 second level school leavers. The original sample of 1985/86 school leavers was subsequently selected for re-interview in late (September–December) 1992, approximately six and a half years after they initially completed their second level education. Of the original sample, 1,659 were successfully traced and most were re-interviewed; though for 432 original respondents — mostly those not living at home — the main "objective" data were provided by parents. Thus, approximately 75 per cent of the original sample and 79 per cent of those first interviewed in May 1987 were successfully traced, and most of these were re-interviewed in 1992. For some of the analyses, however, where data are required directly from respondents, only data from 1,227 (61 per cent) of respondents are used. As there were some slight biases in the response rates of different categories of school leavers (especially early leavers) the

1992 sample is re-weighted to correct for such "objective" biases.[1] The three tables that follow give some indication of the representativeness and characteristics of both samples.

RESPONDENTS' CHARACTERISTICS 1987 AND 1992

First, educational level shows little change between 1987 and 1992 for those leaving school with less than a Leaving Certificate (Table 2.1). Seventy per cent of school leavers had achieved Leaving Certificate level in 1987. Of these, almost 40 per cent went on immediately to third level education, or 28 per cent of the total school-leaving sample. Approximately one-in-seven of these did not successfully complete their course by 1992. While there are no significant gender differences in the overall proportions entering third level, males are far more likely to have left school before the Leaving Certificate — a finding which has held since at least the 1960s.

Table 2.1: Level of Education Achieved by 1985/86 School Leavers in 1987 and 1992 (Percentage)

	1992			1987
Highest Educational Level	*Males*	*Females*	*Total*	*Total*
No Qualifications	8.4	5.3	6.9	7.2
Group/Inter Certificate	27.3	17.9	22.8	22.6
Leaving Certificate	33.4	47.4	40.2	70.2
Incomplete Third Level	6.7	4.7	5.8	–
Certificate/Diploma	11.5	11.3	14.4	–
Degree	12.6	13.3	12.9	–
N	*853*	*806*	*1659*	*2089*

[1] However, there may be unmeasured characteristics which effectively cannot be corrected for. For example non-respondents are higher amongst migrants and particularly emigrants, and their views and attitudes may be different from non-migrants. Most of our analyses, however, are based on the larger (79 per cent) sample, where such sample biases do not appear to be as serious.

Age by 1992 shows some gender differences, as one might expect given that 76 per cent of females completed their Leaving Certificates, compared to 64 per cent of males. The average age for both males and females is almost 24 by late 1992, with 15 per cent of females being 25 and over, compared to seven per cent of males.

Table 2.2: Age of 1985/86 School Leavers in 1992 (percentages); and Age in May 1986

Age in 1992	Males	Females	Total	Age May 1986
19 or 20 Years	1.6	0.8	1.2	< 15
21 or 22 Years	22.0	13.3	17.8	15–16
23 or 24 Years	69.4	71.2	70.3	17–18
25 and Over	7.0	14.7	10.8	19 +
Average Age	*23.6*	*23.7*	*23.6*	*17.2*
Total N	*851*	*805*	*1656*	*2090*

Given the average six and a half year gap between school leaving (mostly in May 1986) and the time of interview in late 1992, the majority of these young people already had extensive labour market experience by the time of the second interview. Those completing full-time education by May 1986 — at Leaving Certificate or lower levels — were over six years in the labour market (see Chapter 3). Associated with this increased labour market experience is an increasing tendency to leave home: almost half (46 per cent) in fact, while over 14 per cent were married and an additional three per cent in permanent "living together" arrangements (see Table 2.3 below).

Table 2.3: Marital Status of 1985/86 School Leavers in 1992

Marital Status	Males %	Females %	Total %
Have been/are Married	8	19	14
Living Together	3	3	3
Single	89	78	83
N	*851*	*805*	*1656*

Both the rate of home leaving and marriage are highly gender- (and age-) related — with females being more likely to leave home (54 per cent vs. 35 per cent), and more than twice as likely to be married. Both of these "leaving home" and marriage patterns are very similar to those observed for the earlier 1982–1987 follow-up survey of school leavers (Hannan and Ó Riain, 1993).

Before we go on to describe the methods used to measure the key variables in our research, we show, in Table 2.4 below, the labour market status of respondents at time of interview in 1992. The results show firstly that, while over 90 per cent of respondents are in the labour market, there are quite significant gender differences in participation. With the exception of those with third level qualifications by 1992, males are more likely to participate — with gender differences being greatest at lowest levels of education. Again, as in the previous 1982–87 follow-up study (Hannan and Ó Riain, 1993), around one-third of young unqualified women have withdrawn from labour force participation — mostly, those with poor labour histories and mostly to "home duties". Female withdrawal declines significantly with increasing level of education — with over 90 per cent of those with a Leaving Certificate or higher being in the labour force. On the other hand, participation is lowest for males amongst those with third level qualifications — almost exclusively due to their higher propensity to remain on in university for longer periods.

Table 2.4: Labour Market Status of Male and Female Respondents by their Level of Education in Late 1992

Labour Market Status	**No Quals**		**Junior Cert.**		**Leaving Cert.**		**Third Level**		**Total**	
	M	*F*	*M*	*F*	*M*	*F*	*M*	*F*	*M*	*F*
1. % in Labour Market	99	70	100	79	98	92	83	89	95	88
2. Of those in the Labour Market:										
(a) % Employed	45	39	73	77	89	93	87	92	81	88
(b) % Unemployed	55	61	27	23	11	7	13	8	19	12

Amongst those in the labour force, unemployment is very unevenly distributed by level of education as well as by gender. If we limit consideration to those in the labour force since leaving school — who did not go on to third level — the unemployment rate is five (for males) to nine times (for females) higher amongst those with "no qualifications" as against those with a Leaving Certificate. So education is crucial to employment chances. In addition, if we exclude the least qualified, males have uniformly higher unemployment rates than females. However, given the higher female withdrawal rates — and the fact that such withdrawal appears to be closely associated with a poor employment history — the overall gender inequality in labour market chances appears unlikely to be male-biased.

KEY VARIABLES

Since one of the main objectives of our research is to assess the extent and nature of the "overlap" in the type and level of jobs taken by third level graduates and those with Leaving Certificate and lower qualifications, the measurement of occupational level achieved and the extent of occupational "overlap" between educational levels, or of "overeducation", is crucial. In both the 1987 and 1992 questionnaires, detailed questions were asked about employment history, from when people first entered the labour force; and about the occupation, industry, size of firm (for current job), part-time or full-time status and permanency, etc., of each job since leaving full-time education. We focus attention on three job types in respondents' work histories: first job, first permanent (or "real") job and current job.

"First Job", First Permanent Job, Current Job

"First job" is defined as the first job taken after respondents completed their full-time education, irrespective of the status or permanency of that job. Paradoxically, the main problem here is not defining "first job", but time of leaving full-time education. For over 90 per cent of respondents, this was unproblematic. Almost all of these either left full-time education in the 1985/86 academic year and never went back on a full-time basis, or else they went on immediately to third level, taking an uninterrupted full-time third level course. Any part-time or vacation jobs they took up while in full-time education, are therefore, ignored. However, a small minority of respondents did not go on immediately to third level after completing their second level education in 1986, but went back one year or more later. In these cases, completing "full-time education" is taken as the date they completed their renewed educational career, and first job is the one following the date they subsequently completed their full-time education. In an even smaller number of cases, respondents entered and left full-time education a number of times. Except in cases, and episodes in a career, where they left for at least two years (where such a long break is taken as equivalent to leaving full-time education) such interrupted educational careers are taken as ended only on the last occasion they completed a full-time educational course before the 1992 interview. "First job", in these cases, refers to a date immediately following such a departure.

"First permanent (or 'real') job" is taken as referring to the first full-time, permanent job respondents had after leaving full-time education; or, if not defined by respondents as permanent, the first full-time job that lasted for a minimum of three months.

"Current job" is defined as the job at time of interview in late October–December 1992.

As already indicated, the great majority of respondents had a very clear-cut, uninterrupted and full-time educational career: leaving second level school in 1985/86 and either directly entering the labour market or going on immediately to a full-time and uninterrupted third level course. Indeed, compared to most other European or other English-speaking countries, Ireland's educational provision and respondent educational careers are very highly structured in this way (see OECD, 1996b: Chapter 3). However, for a small and apparently growing minority, "in-and-out" movements between education and the labour market are quite marked. (We will deal with these variations in detail in a later publication.)

Defining Occupational Level

Since we are primarily interested in the degree of correspondence, or correlation, between level of education achieved and "level of occupation"[2] achieved, conceptualising and measuring "occupational

---

[2] Taking "occupation" (including employer/employee status) — whether categorised in "class" or "status" terms — as measuring the most important aspect of respondent's "position" in the labour market: status, security, degree of

level" is crucial to our exercise. In the Irish case, given the higher degree of vertical differentiation, and low degree of horizontal differentiation, of our educational system (see Hannan *et al.*, 1996) we take "level of education" as being unproblematic — an outcome not characteristic of German-speaking countries or the Netherlands, all of which have significant "horizontal differentiation" in the "type", as well as level, of education and qualification received. "Educational level" is then defined as an ordinal (hierarchical) scale: 1 = "No Qualifications", 2 = Group/Inter Certificate, 3 = Leaving Certificate, 4 = Third Level (mostly RTC) Certificate, 5 = Third Level Diploma, 6 = University Degree, 7 = Higher Degree.

In this research, we define "occupational (or job) level" purely in "occupational status" terms for the following reasons. We are primarily interested in "level congruence" (Allmendinger, 1989) between level of education and level of occupational achievement. Thus, at least an ordinal level of measurement of the status of occupations/jobs achieved is required. "Class" or "social class" concepts and measures, which emphasise important distinctions in the relationships of production, or in employment status — as employer, self-employed, employee, etc. — and other occupational characteristics (Erikson and Goldthorpe, 1992) are not used for two main reasons. The basic class distinction between employer and employee, etc., is not relevant, because almost everyone at this level is an employee. Secondly, class categories are not hierarchically ordered, and in any case do not have sufficient discrimination, aggregating occupations too grossly for our purposes. We could, for instance, use the Irish, six-value, "social class" scale — effectively an occupational status scale. However, there is too little discrimination in this scale to be of use in distinguishing amongst educational levels in the "occupational levels" first achieved.

We therefore use the 36-value Hope-Goldthorpe scale (1974) as an "occupational status" scale for the following reasons, although the authors clearly dislike the term:

- It is the most reliable and valid "occupational status" scale on this side of the Atlantic, although developed for Britain in the

---

autonomy, influence/control over others, opportunities for promotion, etc. Industrial sector or segment will also be dealt with separately, but to a more limited extent, as will wage/salary levels.

early 1970s. The main occupational and employment status categories — for the 36-category version — are so well described that it is relatively straightforward to apply in the Irish case; and has been used previously by Whelan and Whelan (1984). It also provides much wider differentiation in occupational statuses than any alternative.

- In using this scale, we do not assume, nor indeed did the original work on such scales by Duncan and Artis (1951) assume, that such an "occupational status" scale provides a reliable index, on its own, of any individual's or family's prestige or social standing within a community or interpersonal network. Nor do we assume that one can infer from its value for any individual what "the relative chances (are) of experiencing deference, acceptance or derogation in his relationships with members of other categories" — as Hope and Goldthorpe appear to assume is inferable from the use of such "occupational status" scales (Hope and Goldthorpe, 1974: 5). In fact, the original work by Duncan and Artis (1951) specifically tested for such a relationship within a small mid-west American rural community, and found a very low correlation between an individual's "occupational status" and his/her individual rating on an overall "community prestige" scale.

- Such "occupational status" scales, as measures of popular assessments of the general "social standing" or "social desirability" of occupations — as gathered from interviews with a British national sample of respondents in the Hope and Goldthorpe (1974) study — appear to be, by and large, "synthesis assessments" of the "social desirability" of occupations. These occupational assessments are highly predictable from a linear combination (by regression) of four average popular gradings of occupations on the basis of: (a) the standard of living associated with them; (b) the power and influence people having these occupations enjoy over others; (c) the average level of educational qualifications people have or require for them; and (d) their "general value to society" (Hope and Goldthorpe, 1974). In this sense, we could equally define these scales as occupational "socio-economic status" scales. For our purposes, however, we will refer to such scales as "occupational status" scales — a term which one of the authors subsequently agrees to (Erikson and Goldthorpe, 1992: 30, footnote 2), although clearly rejected in the original study (Hope and Goldthorpe, 1974).

We use the reduced 36-value scale. Because of zero or very small numbers in some cells, however, we aggregate these down to 24. These are described in Table 2.5, which also gives the distribution of respondents for "first job", "first permanent job" and "current job"; as well as the "occupational status" scale values for each occupational category.[3] The modal and average occupational status category ranges closely around the intermediate non-manual (clerical, etc.) category for all three jobs — with a slight increase in the average value from 37 for "first job" to 43 for current job — from slightly below to slightly above the scale value for intermediate non-manual (clerical, etc.) workers. The variances are very wide and remain relatively stable — with the lower interquartile range values increasing from 27 (service workers, lower grade) to 35 (intermediate grade service workers) from first job to current job; while the upper interquartile range value increases from 40 to 53. The main upward shifts in the averages and interquartile ranges, however, occur between first permanent job and current job. As can be seen, however, from the decline in the number of people employed, much of this apparent upward shift in occupational status may be due to a disproportionate number of unskilled/semi-skilled manual/service workers losing their first jobs and being unemployed or out of the labour force by late 1992. This issue will be taken up later.

Measuring "Overqualification"

The concept of overqualification implies a pronounced relationship between level of education achieved and status of occupation achieved — the idea of "level congruence" as defined by Allmendinger (1989). In highly standardised and segmented education/training systems, such as the German "dual system", there is a high correlation between both type and level of

---

[3] Scale values are derived from scored responses of a national sample of respondents who are asked to evaluate the general social standing of selected occupational titles on a scale of 1 to 100, the latter being the maximum status value.

Table 2.5: Percentage Distribution of Respondents at Work by Occupational Status — Hope-Goldthorpe Scale: First Job, First Permanent Job, Current Job

Hope-Goldthorpe Scale*			**First Job**	**First Permanent Job**	**Current Job**
No.	*Titles*	*Scale value*	%	%	%
1&2	Higher professionals; self-employed and salaried	71	4.6	5.3	6.5
3	High administrators and officials (higher grade)	69	0.4	0.5	1.2
4&5	Industrial managers — large enterprise; and administrators/officials	65	0.8	1.0	1.0
6	Technicians (higher grade)	63	1.9	2.3	2.8
8&9	Industrial and business managers (small enterprises)	62	5.0	6.4	9.9
10	Salaried professionals (lower grade)	61	0.4	0.5	0.8
11	Farmers and farm managers	58	0.1	0.1	0.4
12&13	Supervisors of non-manual employees (higher grade); and small proprietors	57	0.4	0.5	1.6
14	Managers in services and small administrative units	53	1.0	1.5	2.9
15	Technicians (lower grade)	51	0.4	0.5	0.8
16&17	Supervisors of lower non-manual; and higher manual employees	47	0.1	0.3	0.9
18	Skilled manual workers in manufacturing (higher grade)	46	3.5	3.7	4.1
19&20	Self-employed workers (higher grade); and supervisors of manual employees (lower grade)	42	–	0.1	0.4
21	Non-manual employees in administration and commerce (e.g. clerical)	40	17.1	18.9	21.5
22&23	Skilled manual workers in manufacturing (intermediate); and construction	38	4.1	4.6	4.5

Hope-Goldthorpe Scale*			**First Job**	**First Permanent Job**	**Current Job**
No.	*Titles*	*Scale value*	%	%	%
24&25	Smallholders; and service workers (higher grade)	37	6.2	6.4	5.1
26&27	Semi-skilled manual workers in manufacturing; skilled manual workers in transport, communications and services	36	5.9	7.0	8.6
28&29	Service workers (interm. grade); and self-employed service (interm. grade) workers	35	12.1	9.9	5.7
30	Skilled manual workers in manufacturing (lower grade)	33	3.0	2.9	3.8
31	Agricultural workers	31	–	–	–
32	Semi-skilled manual workers in construction and extractive industries	30	3.7	3.2	2.7
33	Semi-skilled manual workers in transport, communications and services	28	2.7	2.5	2.8
34	Service workers (lower grade)	27	15.8	13.0	7.3
35	Unskilled manual and lower grade service workers	18	10.8	8.9	4.5
	Total N		*1580*	*1528*	*1275*
	%		*100*	*100*	*100*
	Lower Interquartile Range		27	30	35
	Median		36	37	*40*
	Upper Interquartile Range		*40*	*40*	53
	Average Score		37	39	*43*
	Standard Deviation		*13*	*14*	*14*

* There were no respondents occupying jobs comprising Hope-Goldthorpe categories 7 (large proprietors) and 36 (self-employed workers lower grade)

education/training and occupational level and type entered. In systems such as the American one, however, where education is not standardised nor as differentiated, there is a lower level of congruence between type and level of education and occupational category entered (Allmendinger, 1989; Rosenbaum and Kariya, 1991; Schupp *et al.,* 1994). Although Ireland has a highly standardised educational system, the curricular and examination system is not segmented as in Germany, with educational levels and qualifications clearly hierarchically stratified (Hannan *et al.*, 1996; Breen *et al.*, 1995). We would then hypothesise a much higher correlation between both level of education and grades achieved in examination and occupational achievement levels than in the American case (see Breen *et al.*, 1995; Shavit and Müller, 1998).

Assuming that there is a moderate to high correlation between level of education achieved and occupational status of first job achieved, or at least first permanent job, we define "over-qualification" as occurring where respondents with educational level X have an occupational status — for first permanent job — which is more characteristic of persons with an educational level lower than themselves; that is, for instance, at or below the median occupational status of those with an educational level of X–1 (an educational level immediately below the respondent's own). So, those with university degrees will be defined as being "overqualified" for their jobs if the occupational status of these jobs is at or below the median occupational status achieved of those with third level (mainly RTC) diplomas. Similarly, the latter will be defined as overqualified if their occupational statuses are at or below the median of those with third level (mainly RTC) certificates, and so on.

This approach to overqualification is similar to that of most of the American research literature on the subject. Here, the "overqualified" are defined usually as those in an occupational status/category with an educational level above some threshold point — usually one standard deviation above the average number of years received for everybody in that occupational category (see Shockey, 1989; Clogg and Shockey, 1984). Besides the definitional nature of this approach — where overqualification occurs irrespective of how diverse or constricted the occupational distribution of each educational level — the use of years of education to measure educational level achieved makes little sense in the highly standardised Irish case. We have one of the most standardised educational systems in the world and level of education achieved is one of the main variables to which employers pay attention in making employment decisions (Breen *et al.*, 1995). In addition, at least at second level, instead of being a useful measure, years of education may be misleading, in that the higher the number of years spent in (and the older the age at) attaining certain levels of education, the lower the grades achieved in examinations (Hannan *et al.*, 1996). Also, grades have been shown to be almost as important, in employment decisions, as level of education achieved (Breen *et al.*, 1995). So, given its obvious conceptual advantages, we use level of education.

Which job, however, should we use to define this threshold: the first job taken after completing full-time education, the first "permanent" job, or the current job? Most school/college leavers take up temporary and part-time jobs while they "wait around" to search for jobs they consider more appropriate. We define "first job", therefore, as the first full-time, "permanent" job (either self-defined as permanent, or jobs which respondents have had for at least three months) which respondents took up after they completed their full-time education. Since almost all respondents have had more than one job, and this appears to be the first secure job they achieved, we take first job as the one to define the "overqualification" threshold. Table 2.6 shows the median occupational statuses of first permanent job for each educational level.

Table 2.6: Median Occupational Statuses Achieved (Hope, Goldthorpe 1974 scale values) by Level of Education, First Permanent Job

	Level of Education 1992						
	No Quals	*Group/ Inter*	*Leaving Cert.*	*Third Level*			*Total*
				Cert.	*Diploma*	*Degree*	
	Median Occupational Status Value						
First Permanent Job	33	35	37	40	53	62	37

There is a direct correlation between level of education and occupational status achieved, with those with degrees having median status values almost twice that of those with no qualifications or even with a Junior Certificate qualification. The median value increases progressively from the lowest to the highest educational level, with the biggest increases occurring between those with third level certificates and diplomas, and between the latter and those with degrees. As we shall see later, the degree of correlation between level of education and occupational status achieved increases over time in the labour market and with the degree of "overlap" between contiguous levels of education declining over time (see Chapter 4). Here, however, it is clear that, at least by the time of "first permanent job", a clear differentiation has emerged and we use it to define the "overqualification" threshold.

Using the above definition, the (median) occupational status threshold — at or below which respondents will be defined as "overqualified" for their jobs — is a value of 53 for those with degrees, 40 for those with diplomas, 37 for those with certificates and 35 for those with a Leaving Certificate. The differences in medians and distributions are so small between those with lower qualifications that we cannot make meaningful distinctions between them.

Referring back to Table 2.5, we can see that these threshold occupational scale values are conservative ones: for degrees, 53 referring to managers of small service units or administrative units; for certificates, most higher grade service workers; and for Leaving Certificate graduates, intermediate grade service workers like most shop assistants. Table 2.7 summarises these threshold values as well as the percentage of respondents at each educational level who are estimated to have been overqualified or overeducated for their first jobs, first permanent jobs and current jobs (at interview in 1992).

The extent to which college graduates take up "second level jobs" immediately after graduating and entering the labour market is surprisingly high: between 40 and 57 per cent for first job, 29–42 per cent for first permanent job, declining to 18–27 per cent for current job. Almost half of third level graduates initially take up very low status "first jobs" while they are "waiting around" for a serious offer, over 30 per cent for first permanent job, declining to just over 20 per cent for current job. So, up to 1992, at least there is very severe initial competition from third level graduates for what are essentially second level jobs.

Table 2.7: "Overqualification Thresholds" and Percentage "Overqualified" for First Job, First Permanent Job and Current Job, by Educational Level

	Level of Education						
Job Category	*No Quals*	*Junior Cert.*	*Leaving Cert.*	*Third Level*			*Total*
				Cert.	*Diploma*	*Degree*	
	Occupational Status at or Below which Respondents are "Overqualified"						
	0	0	35	37	40	53	–
	Percentage "Overqualified"						
First Job (N=1580)	0	0	47	40	57	43	33
First Permanent Job (N=1528)	0	0	39	31	42	29	26
Current Job (1992) (N=1275)	0	0	26	18	27	21	19

For those with a Leaving Certificate, the position is very similar — competing directly with pre-Leaving Certificate school leavers, even for semi-skilled and unskilled manual/service occupations. Even after six years in the labour market, although there is a substantial decline in "overqualification", over one-in-four of those with a Leaving Certificate are still working in low-skilled manual/service occupations — jobs much more characteristic of those with very low qualification levels. The fall in the percentage "overqualified" from first to current job is proportionately greater for those with a certificate or diploma. Much the same proportion as Leaving Certificate respondents are "overqualified" for current (1992) jobs, though they have spent only around half the time of Leaving Certificate graduates in the labour force. So, on an annualised basis, they are moving upward out of "poor jobs" at a much faster pace than Leaving Certificate respondents. For those with university degrees — who on average are less than two years in the labour market — this decline appears to be equally as rapid from first job to current job. Overqualification, and particularly competition between second and third level graduates, is therefore very prevalent amongst school/college leavers in their first year or two in the labour market. Over time, however, this declines rapidly as third level graduates gradually move upwards out of low status occupations.[4] These patterns will be discussed in detail in Chapter 4.

SUMMARY

This six-year follow-up survey of school leavers is based on late 1992 interviews with 1,659 respondents, over 80 per cent of the original sample who were first interviewed in May/June 1987, one year after they had completed their second level education. Re-weighted, it then provides a reliable sample of the labour market experiences of the total population of school leavers from 1985/86 for their first six years in the labour market. Over 70 per cent of these had a Leaving Certificate or higher qualification, with 27 per cent having a third level one. Almost all had entered the labour market, with the exception of a small percentage of third level entrants who had not yet completed their education. Withdrawal from the labour force was very structured: over 30 per cent of young women with the poorest educational qualifications and poor labour market history, but extremely few of those with good qualifications and good labour market history. Almost no young men, irrespective of qualifications, had withdrawn from labour force participation (see also Hannan and Ó Riain, 1993).

Educational level is an ordinal variable, from a value of one for "no qualifications" — left before taking any junior cycle examination — to a value of seven for those with post-graduate third level (Master's or higher) qualifications. Occupational status is measured using an adaptation of the Hope-Goldthorpe scale (1974), with 36 categories and values ranging from 18 to 72. Overqualification is then defined as occurring when a person with an educational level X has an occupational status value lower than that more typical (at or less than the median value) of those with educational level X–1. That is, in more common-sense terms, college graduates taking up Leaving Certificate jobs; or Leaving Certificate graduates taking up jobs more typical of those with Junior Certificate qualifications or none. As we

---

[4] The fact that third level respondents have fewer years in the labour market means that their upward mobility rate will tend to be underestimated. However, their shorter duration in the labour market does not appear to have any effect on their probability of getting a first permanent job.

saw, such outcomes are very common amongst school/college leavers in their first year or so in the labour market — but with fast upward mobility out of such lower status jobs, level of "overqualification" declines significantly over time. Chapter 4 describes these outcomes in great detail. In the next chapter, we describe in some detail the post-school education, training and labour market history of respondents for the six-year period following their school leaving.

Chapter 3

Educational and Labour Market History

We have two main objectives in this chapter. The first is to describe the post-school educational history of the school-leaving cohort. Second, we describe the early labour market history of these young school/college leavers in their first two to six years in the labour market. As we shall see, this labour market entry process is highly structured by the level of education achieved, the probability of successful employment and (later described) the level of occupation/earnings achieved. The extent to which school/college leavers, with different levels of educational qualifications, compete with each other in the same sectors of the labour market, or the extent to which they enter different sectors, is the subject of the next chapter.

Irish institutional arrangements for education, which structure young people's gradual and cumulative acquisition of educational qualifications, appear to be both more rigid and more hierarchically organised than in many other European countries. Educational provision is almost completely full-time, with little part-time provision leading to the gradual cumulation of marketable qualifications. It is extremely time-bound in two senses. Firstly, in relation to the life cycle, there is a minuscule level of "second chance" education for those who leave early with poor qualifications. Secondly, although such second-chance provision is growing at third level, it is almost exclusively full-time, Monday to Friday, traditional nine-to-five provision. In both senses, therefore, Irish educational provision appears to be mainly determined by conventionalised provider behaviour and interests, and not as obviously by public policy needs. Besides these routinised age- and time-bound provision constraints, the rather inflexible curricular and examination system and the extensive use of examination results in the selection process for further education/training and employment has created an education system which is both rigidly discriminating and rather final in its initial outcomes and judgements on young people graduating from it. Unlike Britain, for instance, it does not facilitate part-time, cumulative credit qualification over a number of years, or provide alternative educational and accreditation channels — such as Further Education Colleges. In addition, the rigid way in which "progression rules" are applied by the state within second level schools militates against progression from one curricular level to another, within or between the junior or senior cycle. This effectively means that young 12/13-year-olds assigned to Foundation or Ordinary curricular levels in their first or second year are effectively limited to such "lower" achievement levels throughout their time in school. Even restricting consideration to English-speaking countries with low provision of institutionalised linkages (such as apprenticeships or occupational specific education/training requirements) between the education/training system and labour market entry (Shavit and Müller, 1998; Müller *et al.*, 1996; Hannan *et al.*, 1996; OECD, 1996b), the Irish education system is a very rigid one with low probability of corrective or "second chance" provision.

POST-SCHOOL EDUCATION AND TRAINING HISTORY

The extent to which further education and training occurs after people complete their initial second level education, and the extent to which education and work institutional arrangements facilitate such flexible re-entry to education, once people have completed their initial education and entered the labour force, has become an increasingly important policy issue in most modern industrialised societies (OECD, 1996b). In the Irish case, however, such subsequent returns to full-time education are rather rare.

As already indicated, these 1985/86 school leavers were first interviewed in May/June 1987, almost a year subsequent to completing their second level education. For many of those who left before taking the Intermediate Certificate examination, however, almost half had left before completing the academic year — particularly those leaving without taking any examination. For both these and other pre-Leaving Certificate school leavers, there is very little subsequent return to full-time education (see Table 3.1 below). Only two per cent of those without any qualifications or with a

Group Certificate ever return to full-time education, or get any subsequent educational qualifications — at least within six years of leaving. And that very small percentage take up their opportunities in the following two years, with a minuscule subsequent return for a "second chance". For those leaving with an Intermediate Certificate, subsequent educational chances are only slightly better — with eight per cent going back to full-time education in subsequent years,

Table 3.1: Percentage Distribution of Respondents by Number of Months in Full-time Education, Post-October 1986 (for full sample, and for those who were not in full-time education in October/November 1986, by level of education (1987))

Number of Months of Full-time Education post-June 1986	**No Quals**	**Group Cert.**	**Inter Cert.**	**Post Inter Cert.**	**Leaving Cert.**
Total Sample	%	%	%	%	%
0	97.9	97.5	92.0	94.1	45.4
1–3	0.7	–	0.8	–	1.2
4–10	0.7	2.5	5.5	1.1	15.1
11–23	0.7	–	1.1	4.7	10.6
24–36	–	–	0.6	–	8.6
37–48	–	–	–	–	8.7
48+	–	–	–	–	10.3
Total %	*100*	*100*	*100*	*100*	*100*
N	*116*	*85*	*229*	*70*	*1154*
For those not in Full-time Education in October/November 1986	%	%	%	%	%
0	99.3	99.2	96.9	99.1	90.9
1–3	0.7	–	0.9	–	1.4
4–10	–	0.8	1.5	–	2.5
11–23	–	–	0.7	0.9	2.2
24+		–	–	–	3.0
Total %	*100*	*100*	*100*	*100*	*100*
N	*114*	*84*	*217*	*66*	*577*

though not generally in ordinary second level schools. But this slightly better performance slackens off, so that by October 1988 (two years later) their subsequent educational chances decline to much the same low level of "second chance" education as those leaving earlier (see second panel of Table 3.1). However, for those with a Leaving Certificate (who do not go on immediately to third level), around one-in-three subsequently go on to take some full-time education/ training course.

Table 3.1 shows the data very clearly, by and large indicating the extraordinary rigidity of the Irish further education system. If one doesn't continue full-time education immediately upon completing second level, subsequent chances of recovery are slim indeed, particularly for the most poorly educated. This time-constraint or restriction on going back to full-time education is described in the table. This indicates firstly the total number of months of post-second-level education received by school leavers for the full six years of observation; but also the even more limited extent to which such education is available/possible if one does not proceed immediately after completing second level.

These figures show a number of clear trends:

- If one completes second level education before Intermediate Certificate, the chances of getting any further education are minimal — around three per cent. If one does not go on almost immediately (i.e. by October 1986) the chances are even more remote. Less than one per cent of those with no qualifications or with Group Certificate qualifications, who did not go on immediately, ever got any further education; and of these, almost all got less than one year's education.

- The chances are only slightly better for those with an Inter Certificate. Eight per cent got some further education — particularly if they went on immediately to some post-second-level course. These courses are roughly split between those of one and two years' duration. Again, if school leavers did not go on immediately, they reduced their chances considerably: only three per cent of those not going on directly in the following academic year (1986/87) ever went back subsequently. Again, these later courses are roughly evenly split between one and two years' duration.

- For those with a Leaving Certificate, however, the situation is considerably better. Just over half of those in total took post-second-level education/training courses — mostly third level. Sixteen per cent took a one-year (i.e. academic year) course or less, 11 per cent a one- to two- year course, nine per cent a course of two to three years, and 19 per cent a course of over three years. Some of the courses were taken up subsequently, or initial post-second-level courses were added on to by subsequently going on to take third level ones. Most of these upper second level leavers, however, went on immediately to further full-time education/training after completing second level; 44 out of the total 55 per cent. The remainder delayed for some time, coming back into full-time education later. Even amongst those with a Leaving Certificate, however, there is very little delayed "return" to full-time education. It is an extremely rigid time- and age-bound system from the perspective of the potential student — particularly the poorly educated student.

Post School Vocational Training

The separately organised vocational training system — by FÁS, CERT, TEAGASC, BIM, Community Training Workshops, etc. — appears, in many respects, to have developed to fill the gaps left by the institutionally rigid second and third level system. Certainly, in terms of providing a complementary vocational training and work experience addition to initial educational qualifications, such post-school full-time training has some egalitarian effects: the lower the level of initial education, the greater the chances of receiving such training. We need to be cautious, however, both about the real educational/training supplementary value of these courses — since many of the FÁS courses are provided mainly to those who are unemployed, and have no clear qualification outcomes. In addition, the extent to which such qualifications growth, when present, is effectively corrective needs to be examined. Given these qualifications, however, the following results show a clear redistributive effect of such post-school training.

Table 3.2: Percentage Distribution of Respondents who Left Full-time Education in 1986 by Number of Months of Full-time Training Subsequently Received by Level of Initial Education (sample refers to those not in full-time education in October or November 1986)

Number of Months of Full-time Vocational Training	**Level of Education**					
	No Quals	*Group Cert.*	*Inter Cert.*	*Post Inter Cert.*	*Leaving Cert.*	*Total*
	%	%	%	%	%	%
1. None	61.2	74.2	77.1	77.7	78.4	75.9
2. 1–3 mths	5.1	7.1	0.9	–	5.3	4.2
3. 4–6 mths	5.2	11.4	8.7	10.1	7.0	7.7
4. 7–12 mths	16.8	3.3	9.3	7.3	7.1	8.3
5. More than 12 mths	11.6	4.0	4.1	4.9	2.3	3.9
Total %	*100*	*100*	*100*	*100*	*100*	*100*
Total N	*114*	*84*	*217*	*66*	*577*	*1059*

While almost 40 per cent of those with no qualifications took such courses — 28 per cent took courses of over six months — this was true of 22 per cent of those with a Leaving Certificate. And in the latter case, these courses were less likely to be long-term ones.

Such a clear redistributive effect is, of course, in keeping with state policy, particularly for those FÁS or other state-financed training courses, which were set up to provide vocational training or work experience for poorly qualified, unemployed youth. Despite this bias toward the unqualified, they are only as likely to have received some nationally recognised certificate for successfully completing a vocational training programme as others — the slight percentage differences present not being statistically significant (Table 3.3). Although only a modest improvement in their qualifications, such vocational training opportunities are, however, clearly both more readily provided and certified than is true for educational provision. Whether such additional vocational training qualifications have any substantial value in the labour market will be explored later.

In summary, therefore, post-school educational provision for pre-Leaving Certificate school leavers is extremely limited (see Table 3.3). And what provision there is, is not redistributive. For "non-college-bound" youth with a Leaving Certificate, however, a surprising third of them receive some further education, and over half receive either education or training.

Table 3.3: Summary of Relationships between Initial (1986) Educational Achievements, Subsequent Education and Training Outcomes

	Level of Education 1986			
	No Quals	*Junior Cycle Quals*	*Leaving Certificate*	*Third Level Entry*
1. Percentage took Subsequent Educational Courses	2	6	34	100
2. Percentage took Vocational Training Course	39	24	22	4
3. Percentage Received Post-School Qualifications	17	9	11	91

Completion of Full-time Education and Entry to the Labour Market

Given these differences in post-second-level education and training, the movement out of education into the labour market is quite spread out over time — the timing of entry dependent mainly on whether respondents went on to third level education. This differentiated pattern is illustrated in Figure 3.1, where the completion of post-second-level educational participation (subsequent to June 1986) is plotted, by level of education, from October 1985 to October 1992.

It is clear that a significant proportion of pre-Leaving Certificate respondents left full-time education before the end of the final 1985/86 session. Most of those without any qualifications left before the exams came up, while those with Group/Intermediate Certificate qualifications who left early did so mainly after participation in a post-examination VPT1 course, or had stayed on for part of a session after completing their examination (though this is less characteristic of those with the Group Certificate).

Figure 3.1: Percentage in Full-time Education by Level of Education, Post Second Level, October 1986 to October 1992

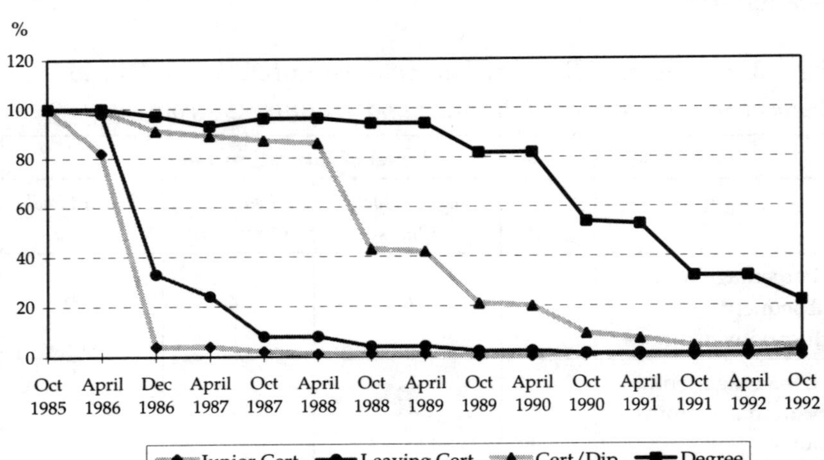

For those with a Leaving Certificate, the overall patterns are similar — though subsequent participation in post-secondary education is significantly greater than for those starting off with lower levels of education. Over 30 per cent of those with a Leaving Certificate — and not directly going on to third level — enter full-time education (with some vocational/training element) during the following (1986/87) academic year. This declines to ten per cent for 1987/88, and between five and seven per cent for 1988/89 to 1989/90. Some of the latter have gone back to third level education. So, for up to three years subsequent to completing their Leaving Certificate, a significant minority continue to attend full-time post-second-level education courses, though not generally in third level courses.

As one would expect, those going on to third level education after successfully completing their Leaving Certificate examinations have quite different patterns. Almost all are still in full-time education at the end of the 1986/87 academic year. (A small number of those who originally were recorded as being in full-time third level education in May/June 1987, but who subsequently dropped out, did not report themselves as having attended third level in 1992.) By the beginning of the second (1987/88) academic year, however, almost 20 per cent of RTC entrants had not returned to college; and by the end of the second (1987/88) academic year, over 50 per cent had either left or completed their courses. This increased to 70 per cent at the end of the third year, 80 per cent at the end of the fourth (1990/91) year; and to 90 per cent at the end of the fifth year. So it would appear that less than one-in-three of those originally starting off on RTC certificate/ diploma courses stayed on to do a three- to four-year degree course.

The initial "drop-out" rate from university courses appears to be much less than from RTCs — particularly in year two (1987/88). When almost 20 per cent of RTC entrants left after the first year, the figure for University entrants was only ten per cent by the end of second year. By the end of the third year, however — by which time a significant proportion would have done their Bachelor degree examinations — almost 30 per cent had left, and by the end of the fourth year, almost 60 per cent — increasing to over 80 per cent by the end of the sixth year.

As to those Leaving Certificate respondents who did not immediately go on to third level courses in 1986/87, just over ten per cent (10.5 per cent) subsequently went on to third level, most of these in the following year. But of those with junior cycle qualifications, less than one per cent went on to take third level courses within the following six years.

Given these initial educational achievement differences, and their relative stability over time, what is the relationship between initial educational achievement and subsequent labour market entry and history characteristics? This we summarise in the following sections.

LABOUR MARKET HISTORY

Most of the 1985/86 school leaving cohort, who did not go on to third level, gradually entered the labour market and got their first jobs over the year from August 1986 to June 1987.

In the following table (Table 3.4) we provide a breakdown of school leavers by their educational and employment status for two periods each year from the end of October 1985 (when 90 per cent were still in school) to October 1992. The information is provided for each of three levels of education achieved by the end of 1992: (a) those who had completed their education before taking the Leaving Certificate examination (N = 492); (b) those who had completed the Leaving Certificate only, or a small number (c. 80) who had gone on

Table 3.4: Percentage Distribution of School Leavers by their Educational and Employment Status (from October/November 1985 to October 1992, for each educational level achieved by late 1992)

Status by Date	Level of Education 1992											
	Pre-Leaving Cert. (N=500)				*Leaving Cert. Incl. Third Level Dropouts (N=761)*				*Third Level Graduates (N=393)*			
	FT Educ. (1)	*At Work or FT Training (2+3)*	*Unemployed (4)*	*Other (5+6+7)*	*FT Educ. (1)*	*At Work or FT Training (2+3)*	*Unemployed (4)*	*Other (5+6+7)*	*FT Educ. (1)*	*At Work or FT Training (2+3)*	*Unemployed (4)*	*Other (5+6+7)*
Oct. '85	97	3	1	–	100	–	–	–	100	–	–	–
May '86	73	19	7	2	97	3	–	–	100	–	–	–
Oct. '86	3	70	23	4	28	55	15	2	93	6	1	–
May '87	3	78	16	3	23	65	11	1	91	9	–	–
Oct. '87	1	76	19	4	8	82	8	1	92	7	1	1
May '88	1	75	20	4	7	85	7	1	91	8	1	1
Oct. '88	1	76	19	5	4	88	6	2	71	25	3	1
May '89	–	76	18	6	3	88	6	3	70	27	2	1
Oct. '89	–	76	17	7	2	90	5	3	54	42	2	2
May '90	–	76	17	7	2	89	6	3	53	44	1	1
Oct. '90	1	74	18	8	1	89	6	3	33	59	5	3
May '91	–	72	20	8	1	88	7	3	31	64	4	1
Oct. '91	–	70	22	9	1	89	6	3	19	71	8	2
May '92	–	65	26	9	1	89	7	3	19	74	5	2
Time of Interview	–	62	29	9	2	87	8	4	13	78	9	1

to third level but failed to complete it (N = 763); and (c) those who had completed a third level course and got a third level qualification — at certificate, diploma or degree level (N = 404), or were still engaged at their studies by the end of 1992. We re-interviewed 81 per cent of the original (N = 2,046) sample in late 1992 and this achieved sample is reweighted to accord with the main characteristics of the original sample.

As can be seen, almost all were still in school in October 1985 — with the exception of a small number of pre-Junior Certificate leavers (almost all boys) who appear to have turned up only for their registration. By the following May (1986), however, over one-in-four of those in pre-Leaving Certificate classes had already left, some, however, having completed the Junior Certificate examination in the preceding year. But at Leaving Certificate level and higher, almost all were still at school — though a small number of those with a Leaving Certificate were at work.

Almost all of those who had completed third level education by 1992 had started off this education in late 1986, though a small proportion subsequently entered third level but were in the labour market in late 1986. Over one-in-four of those who finished their education at Leaving Certificate level were in other (non-third-level) full-time education/training courses in late 1986 to early 1987, and even four per cent of pre-Leaving Certificate leavers. So, one year after completing their second level education, almost half of those who did the Leaving Certificate were still in full-time education or training — mostly in third level. Only four per cent of those with less than a Leaving Certificate were so engaged.

By October 1987 and until May 1988 — two years after completing their second level education — over 90 per cent of those who went on immediately to third level were still so engaged. A similar situation also held for six to seven per cent of those who completed their initial education at Leaving Certificate stage (most in "two and a half level" courses). So, while almost all of those who completed their second level education at pre-Leaving Certificate level directly entered the labour market upon leaving school, almost half of those completing the Leaving Certificate still remained in full-time education or training one year later and around one-third two years later.

However, by two and a half to three years later (October 1988 to May 1989), almost one-third (30 per cent) of those originally going to third level had left, the great majority having successfully completed their two- to three-year courses — though three per cent of initial Leaving Certificate graduates were still in full-time education, some amongst them being "returnees".

Four years later — May 1990 — the proportion of original third level entrants still in college was down to half; five years later (May 1991), to a third, and six years later (October 1992), to 13 per cent. So, there is a long drawn-out process of furthering their education amongst those originally more qualified; with most (though not all) third level entrants going on immediately to third level after successfully completing their Leaving Certificate. A small number (about ten per cent) of Leaving Certificate graduates enter third level later after spending some time in the labour market. But a substantial proportion of those with only a Leaving Certificate do take other post-Leaving education and vocational/technical courses. If we cumulate those who took VPT/PLC courses before leaving full-time education with those who subsequently went on to take post-second-level full-time educational, vocational training courses (FÁS, CERT, Teagasc, BIM, etc.) the percentages come to 42 per cent for those with a Leaving Certificate, and almost 40 for those with junior cycle or no qualifications. So there is a very substantial amount of full-time, in-school and post-school, educational and vocational training being given to "non-college-bound" youth: though only around a third of these courses appear to have led to marketable qualifications.

Timing of First Jobs

Almost all of those (93 per cent) who completed their education at pre-Leaving Certificate level in 1985/86 entered the labour market immediately on leaving school, with over one-in-four entering before the end of the 1985/86 school year. Employment maximises (at 78 per cent) one year later in May 1987 — and stays relatively steady for the following three years (May 1990); after which it declines steadily, with unemployment increasing up to time of interview. This is clearly illustrated in Figure 3.2. Labour market entry for Leaving Certificate "leavers" is more spread out initially, with many (one-in-four) remaining in full-time education/training for up to one year. So it is late 1987 by the time their employment levels reach those of junior cycle leavers (see Figure 3.2). Unlike the latter, however, their employment chances improve significantly with time in the labour market, significantly fewer withdrawing from the labour market. This contrast in employment history is clearly illustrated in Figure 3.2.

For those going on to RTC certificate/diploma courses in October 1986, labour market entry starts in mid-1988, two years later, and grows rapidly thereafter, reaching Leaving Certificate levels by late 1990 (see Figure 3.2). For those on degree courses, labour market entry only starts seriously four years after entry. It grows steadily thereafter until the time of interview in late 1992, when there were still over 20 per cent in full time education, six years after completing their second level education (see Figure 3.2).[1]

Figure 3.2: Percentage "At Work" by Level of Education (October 1986 to October 1992)

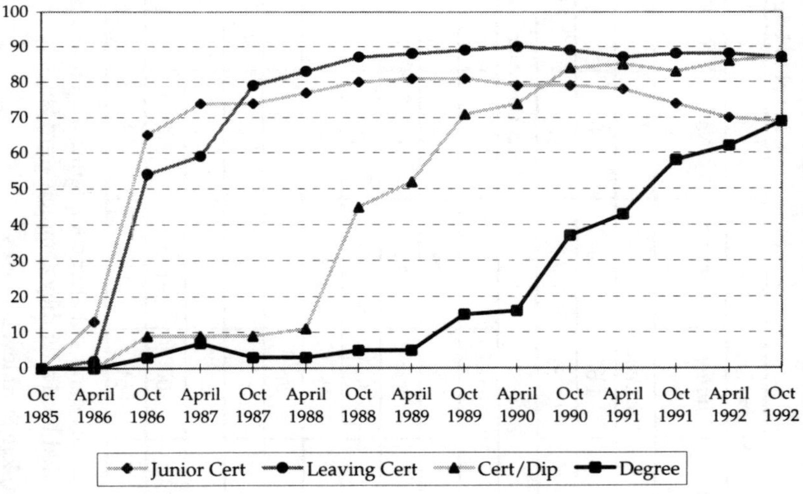

The job history of those who initially left full-time education at or before Leaving Certificate level in 1985/86 is given in Table 3.5.

[1] Figures 3.1 and 3.2 are based on level of education completed by end 1992 — and for those categorised as third level, a small proportion did not enter immediately upon completing their second level education in 1986 — hence the small proportion at work from October 1986 to October 1989.

Table 3.5: Time (Year) of First Job amongst 1985/86 Second Level School Leavers; by Level of Education Achieved in 1992*

	Level of Education 1992								
	Second Level			*Third Level*					
Time of First Job	*Pre Junior Cert*	*Junior Cert*	*Leaving Cert*	*No Quals***	*Certificate*	*Diploma*	*Bachelors Degree*	*Postgrad. Degree*	*Total*
	Per Cent			*Per Cent*					
None as of late 1992	21.1	4.6	1.4	3.0	1.2	6.1	16.6	23.1	6.6
(N)	(111)	(378)	(667)	(96)	(114)	(75)	(173)	(42)	(1659)
	Percentage of those with at least one Job								
1985	15	3	7	–	–	–	–	–	1
1986	38	55	54	5	7	1	2	–	39
1987	31	32	34	63	17	–	3	–	29
1988	9	5	8	20	46	24	3	–	11
1989	4	3	3	9	22	53	19	3	9
1990	3	1	–	1	6	16	39	22	6
1991	–	1	1	1	2	6	23	44	4
1992	–	–	–	1	–	–	11	31	2
Total %	100	100	100	100	100	100	100	100	100
N	90	361	658	93	113	70	144	32	1550

* First job is defined as the first job respondents got after completing their initial period of education. Students who take a year out before going on to third level are not included until after they complete third level.

** Those who failed or did not complete third level courses.

Roughly half of those with a Leaving Certificate or Group/ Intermediate Certificate got jobs in the 1986 calendar year — mostly between June and December of that year. Those with a Leaving Certificate got first jobs over a longer period: 42 per cent not getting first jobs until 1987/88, compared to 35 per cent for those with a junior cycle qualification. This is primarily due to the greater proportion of Leaving Certificate leavers in full-time education/ training in 1986/87. Those with no qualifications have an even more extended period of absorption into the labour force, with around one-in-five never getting a job at all. The equivalent proportion with no jobs after six years amongst those with Junior or Leaving Certificate qualifications is less than three per cent.

The median, and modal, year of getting a first job is 1986 for all second level leavers. A small proportion (15 per cent) of pre-JC leavers had left school and got a job before the end of the 1985/86 school session. For those entering third level but dropping out, or failing, the equivalent median year is 1987. Obviously, most dropped out or failed after one year. For those with a certificate qualification, the median year for a first job is 1988 — after two years of study — and 1989 for those with a diploma — after three years of study. Interestingly, in these latter three cases, their labour market entry, or first job, timings are much more spread out than for second level leavers. And this time spread on entry to first job is even more extended for those with either a Bachelor's or post-graduate university degree. Modal entry year is four years later for Bachelor's, and five years for postgraduate degrees. For all third level graduates, however, it is clear that a small minority actually worked for some time prior to entering third level courses. Not represented in the above figures, for instance, because of the way "first job" is calculated (only after they have graduated), over 15 per cent of third level graduates had worked full time in 1986/87.

We summarise the relationships between educational level achieved and labour market experience in Table 3.6. In order to get an overall picture of those with relatively similar labour market exposure, we restrict consideration to those who directly entered the labour market in 1986 — excluding those who immediately went on to further full-time education or training. We first describe their average period of time in the labour market and its breakdown into time employed and unemployed for each level of education.

Table 3.6: Average Time (Number of Months) in Labour Market, and Time Employed and Unemployed, for each Educational Level (in 1987) (of those who left school and directly entered the labour market in 1986 and were re-interviewed in 1992)

Of Those Ever in Labour Market 1986–92	**Level of Education (1987)**					
	No Quals	*Group Cert.*	*Inter Cert.*	*Post Inter Cert.*	*Leaving Cert.*	*Total*
Average Amount of Time in Labour Market	69.6	72.7	69.6	72.6	70.2	70.3
(Standard Deviation)	*(14.7)*	*(10.9)*	*(16.2)*	*(13.3)*	*(12.8)*	*(13.7)*
Total N	*114*	*84*	*217*	*66*	*586*	*1063*
	(p = ns)					
Average Amount of Time Employed	39.8	59.3	57.5	59.4	63.1	59.0
(Standard Deviation)	*(31.3)*	*(20.9)*	*(23.5)*	*(22.3)*	*(18.2)*	*(22.6)*
Total N	*114*	*84*	*217*	*66*	*583*	*1067*
	(F = 15.4; p<.001)					
Average Amount of Time Unemployed	28.8	13.4	11.9	11.4	7.1	11.1
(Standard Deviation)	*(30.0)*	*(19.0)*	*(17.6)*	*(16.7)*	*(13.1)*	*(18.4)*
Total N	*114*	*84*	*217*	*66*	*583*	*1067*
	(F = 15.4; p<.001)					

As can be clearly seen, there are only very small (and statistically insignificant) differences amongst the different education levels in the time spent in the labour market — on average just over 70 months. There are substantial differences, however, in the time spent employed and unemployed. While those without qualifications spent almost 30 months unemployed — almost three times the average level, those with junior cycle qualifications spent around 12 to 13 months, and those with a Leaving Certificate only seven months. So an extremely clear pattern of labour market disadvantage occurs. While those with a Leaving Certificate spent only ten per cent of their time unemployed, those without any qualifications spent an average of 41 per cent. The average amount of time employed correspondingly increases: from 40 months out of 70 for those without qualifications, to 63 out of 70 for those with a Leaving Certificate — over 50 per cent higher than the former. So employment chances are highly dependent on level of education achieved.

Besides the amount of time spent employed or unemployed, the number of jobs or periods of unemployment experienced provides equally illuminating information on employment security. Tables 3.7 and 3.8 contain the relevant data.

Table 3.7: Percentage Distribution by Number of Jobs to October 1992 (of those not in full-time education in October/November 1986)

Of Those who Left School in 1985/86 and did not go on to full-time Education	**Level of Education (1986)**					
	No Quals	*Group Cert.*	*Inter Cert.*	*Post Inter Cert.*	*Leaving Cert.*	*Total*
Number of Jobs	%	%	%	%	%	%
0	23	1	4	5	1	4
1	31	27	23	15	24	24
2	20	34	22	19	30	27
3	17	21	24	28	23	23
4	6	12	15	24	10	11
5+	3	5	12	10	13	11
Total %	*100*	*100*	*100*	*100*	*100*	*100*
N	*114*	*84*	*217*	*66*	*577*	*1059*
Average Number of Jobs	1.6	2.3	2.8	2.8	2.3	2.3
(Standard Deviation)	(1.3)	(1.2)	(1.4)	(1.3)	(1.3)	(1.4)
Average No. of Jobs p.a.	0.29	0.40	0.47	0.46	0.46	0.44

Complete failure to get any job at all is a serious problem only for those who left school without any qualifications — with almost one-in-four without any job. For others, the figure runs between one and five per cent. As a result, the average number of jobs held by those with no qualifications is substantially lower than others, at 1.6. There is little difference amongst other educational groups in the number of jobs held — varying only between 2.3 and 2.8 jobs on average.

These figures on job numbers are substantially lower than equivalent ones quoted for the United States and Canada — and much closer to the British and European pattern (OECD, 1996b). So, the labour market for Irish youth in terms of the extent of "job shopping" behaviour by young people entering it, is much more stable or less turbulent than recent reports of the American youth labour market indicate, where young people spend a long time in short-term jobs searching for first "real" jobs (see OECD, 1996b: 118–126). If we take average annual number of jobs (per year in the labour market), then those without qualifications = 0.29; Intermediate Certificate = 0.47; and Leaving Certificate = 0.46. These figures are almost identical to the British ones and almost half those for the United States (OECD, 1996b: 126). The underlying reasons for these differences between the US and European countries (and Japan) may be related to the lack of standardisation of American high school education and qualifications, the weaker institutional linkages between school/training and labour market entry, as well as the highly unregulated nature of the American labour market. The authors of the OECD review, on the other hand, suggest the influence of an equally valuable and more variable set of work experiences of American youth in a rapidly changing labour market (OECD, 1996b: 126).

As we have already seen, there is a very clear relationship between unemployment, length of unemployment and educational level: those without any qualifications experience more than four times as much unemployment on average as those with a Leaving Certificate. This unemployment experience is a function both of the number of spells of unemployment — which tend to be larger — and the average spell length. The following table shows the number of unemployment spells.

Table 3.8: Number of Periods of Unemployment to November 1992 (of those entering the labour market in 1986)

Number of Unemployment Periods	**Level of Education (1986)**					
	No Quals	*Group Cert.*	*Inter Cert.*	*Post Inter Cert.*	*Leaving Cert.*	*Total*
	%	%	%	%	%	%
0	29	38	43	36	51	45
1	38	40	27	38	31	32
2	17	16	17	13	13	14
3+	16	7	13	14	6	9
Total %	*100*	*100*	*100*	*100*	*100*	*100*
Total N	*114*	*84*	*217*	*66*	*577*	*1059*
Average Number	*1.3*	*1.1*	*1.2*	*1.2*	*0.8*	

The data show a very clear pattern of decreasing unemployment spells with increasing educational levels. Half of those with a Leaving Certificate had no unemployment, less than one-third had one period and 19 per cent had two or more periods. This contrasts sharply with the experience of the least qualified — where only 29 per cent experienced no unemployment, almost 40 per cent had one period and 33 per cent had two or more periods. However, the differences amongst the four groups with less than a Leaving Certificate are insignificant in these respects; though, as we can see from Table 3.6, the amount of time spent unemployed by those without any qualifications is more than twice that of those with junior cycle qualifications, and over four times greater than those with a Leaving Certificate. So it appears that it is not the number of spells of unemployment that distinguishes these "early leavers" from each other, but the 23 per cent who never got a job, as well as the greater average length of the spells.

Besides the number and length of spells of unemployment, the length of time taken to get one's first job after completing initial education is one of the main constituents of the unemployment experience — not least because previous labour market history is such an important criterion in subsequent employment experience. In keeping with previous research, we would expect that the lower the educational level, the longer this initial waiting period for the first job. The results presented in Table 3.9 provide support for this hypothesis, even ignoring those who never got any job and had effectively withdrawn from the labour market by 1992. This fate is suffered almost exclusively by those without any qualifications. There is, however, still a strong tendency for the least qualified to have taken a longer time to get their first job — 44 per cent of them having got it in less than four months, compared to 56 per cent of those with a Leaving Certificate. At the other extreme, 41 per cent of the least qualified and only 22 per cent of those with a Leaving Certificate took over a year to get their first job.

Table 3.9: Amount of Time to First Job, of Those Who Got a Job (for those completing initial education in 1986 and entering labour market)

Amount of Time Between Leaving School and First Job	**Level of Education (1986)**					
	No Quals	*Group Cert.*	*Inter Cert.*	*Post Inter Cert.*	*Leaving Cert.*	*Total*
	%	%	%	%	%	%
(1) 1 month or less	42	35	36	57	37	38
(2) 2–3 months	2	7	14	9	19	15
(3) 4–6 months	6	9	8	1	10	9
(4) 6–12 months	10	24	19	17	12	15
(5) 13–24 months	25	15	17	7	19	18
(6) 25–36 months	8	6	6	6	2	4
(7) Over 3 years	8	4	1	3	1	2
Total %	*100*	*100*	*100*	*100*	*100*	*100*
N	*91*	*83*	*206*	*63*	*567*	*1,010*
Average Number of Months	*8.9*	*7.8*	*7.7*	*5.5*	*5.8*	*7.1*

So the least qualified have the highest probability of never being employed; suffer by far the longest period of unemployment; take much longer to get their first job; but nevertheless have more and longer spells of unemployment. In almost all of these respects, the overall labour market chances of those with a Leaving Certificate are between four times better (the period unemployed) to almost twice as advantaged (number of unemployment periods) as those with no qualifications. Educational qualifications are therefore of crucial significance in the Irish youth labour market. Whether one explains such results in "human capital" theory terms — in the absence of crucial basic skills (of literacy and numeracy for instance) which are generally accurately indexed (though not fully) by such examination results (see Bynner, 1996) — or whether "screening/queuing" theories are more useful conceptual tools, cannot be adequately tested here. Both, however, would predict much higher levels of unemployment amongst the least qualified. The rapid growth over time in the educational qualifications of those within the same occupational category — even of the least skilled categories — would suggest, within the Irish context at least, that "queuing/screening" theories have significant utility (see Sexton *et al.*, 1996; Breen *et al.*, 1995; Hannan *et al.*, 1996; Breen, 1984a; Hannan, 1986).

The rigidity or lack of responsiveness of the educational system to initial underachievement is quite remarkable — "second chances" have very low probabilities. Vocational training courses and work experience schemes are, on the other hand, quite redistributive, but appear to yield few marketable qualifications. Given the extent of overcrowding in the Irish labour market and the extent to which employers use educational credentials in appointment decisions (Breen *et al.*, 1995), the quite biased distribution of unemployment is not unexpected. Given these results, one would expect substantial competition between educational levels for jobs and significant "overlaps" in occupational status distributions between closely related educational levels — e.g. between those with a university degree and those with an RTC diploma, or between those with an RTC certificate and those with a Leaving Certificate. This issue will be explored in detail in the following chapter.

SUMMARY

The results indicate a high degree of institutional rigidity in the Irish educational system, particularly for those leaving early with poor qualifications. For those, it almost appears as if the full-time educational system has expelled them — giving almost no opportunity for second chances. Recent curricular and examination reforms do appear to have had positive results — in terms of greater retention to examination levels, as well as a lower level of examination failure. These appear in general to have had positive educational and labour market effects (Hannan and McCoy, 1995). However, for those who leave without qualifications or with poor junior cycle ones, there appears to have been little change and, given the level of alienation of such ex-pupils from educational providers (Hannan and Ó Riain, 1993), it would require much more fundamental change than has occurred to provide effective second-chance education for them. Post-school vocational training, however, has been more successful, with up to one-in-four of the most poorly qualified improving their vocational training qualifications.

For those with a Leaving Certificate or higher qualification, however, post-school education is immeasurably better. Over a third of those entering the labour market directly take post-school courses — mostly VPT or PLC courses — though at that stage most of these did not lead to additional qualifications. Since 1992, however, there have been significant improvements in these respects. Of third level entrants in 1986/87, almost 90 per cent graduated, and for these there was ample further educational provision.

Entry into the labour market is almost immediate for pre-Leaving Certificate leavers — with less than five per cent never entering the labour market at all. Employment stabilises at almost 80 per cent for these after one year, with unemployment and withdrawal from the labour force growing significantly, however, after five years or so. Withdrawal is most characteristic of females, unemployment of males. Such poorly qualified youth, therefore, not only have greater difficulty in initial labour market absorption, but also have far greater probability of subsequently falling out of employment. For those with a Leaving Certificate qualification, absorption is at first slower — due mainly to their greater education/training involvement, but maximises to a much higher level — at around 90 per cent after two years. Unemployment is always lower and declines with no evidence of increasing again within the following five to six years. For third level graduates, labour market entry is much more spread out, in keeping with the phasing of their graduation — reaching one-in-four after three years and three-out-of-four after five years. Unemployment at any stage is very low for them, and appears to be mainly a temporary entry problem.

Expressed in terms of the proportion of time in the labour market spent unemployed, the unemployment experience is more than four times greater for the least qualified. The poorly educated are much more likely never to get a job, taking much longer to get one, with shorter periods in keeping one, and much longer periods of unemployment, with the number of jobs being roughly equal across all educational groups. Anticipating some of the results of the following chapters, it is almost as if there is a relatively stable stock of poorly skilled "youth jobs", access to which is highly dependent on level of education, with the most poorly educated being either initially excluded or, if included, gradually losing out again as later cohorts enter the system, or as labour market prospects decline.

Chapter 4

Comparing Occupations Entered According to Educational Level

In this chapter, we describe in some detail the nature and extent to which second and third level school/college leavers take up the same or similar occupations. The concept of "overqualification" essentially refers to the extent to which those with higher levels of qualification (such as university graduates) take jobs/occupations that they could have achieved without their degrees or diplomas, or that those with Leaving Certificate qualifications have achieved. Both state and individual expectations would be that college graduates should get "better" jobs — in terms of skill levels, responsibility, autonomy, status and income levels, etc. At this point, we pay attention only to the "occupational status" of the job. We will later examine earnings and job/industrial sector. As we saw in Chapters 2 and 3, those entering the labour market directly from second level education had an average of two to three jobs in their first five or six years in the labour market and that there is considerable "overlap" in the first occupations taken up.

In this chapter, we firstly describe the extent and nature of that "overlap" in the occupations entered by school leavers with different levels of education. We use the Hope-Goldthorpe occupational status scale (1974) to measure occupational "quality", and we first use Duncan's index of dissimilarity to measure overlap. This measures the extent to which two columns of proportions — say, the proportions of those with a Leaving Certificate qualification and those with less than that level — in a range of occupational categories are similar to or differ from each other. The measure varies from a value of 0.0, where the two distributions are exactly the same, to a value of 1.0, where the two distributions are completely different. The latter would hold where, for example, all Leaving Certificate leavers have occupations of at least intermediate non-manual level (most clerical, "white collar" jobs), and where all of those with less than a Leaving Certificate have occupations of a lower status — say most manual and lower status service occupations.

Secondly, we detail the substantial changes in occupational status levels from first job to current job, particularly amongst those with third level qualifications, as well as changes in the distribution of these jobs. As we have already seen, there is substantial upward mobility out of lower status jobs amongst third level leavers in their first years at work. As a result, although there is a high degree of overlap in first jobs/occupations entered by those with different levels of education, this appears to decline rapidly with time in the labour force. This issue of "overqualification" and its changes over time in the labour market is dealt with in detail in the final section of the chapter.

DEGREE OF OCCUPATIONAL SIMILARITY/DISSIMILARITY AMONGST THOSE WITH DIFFERENT LEVELS OF EDUCATION

We first measure occupational "overlap" using the traditional and comprehensive measure of degree of "dissimilarity" between two occupational distributions — of, for example, two contrasting educational levels. This is the conventional "Duncan dissimilarity" index (Duncan and Duncan, 1955):

$$D = ½ \sum_{i} [P_{i1} - P_{i2}],$$

where P_{i1} = the proportion of workers in occupational status i with educational level 1, and P_{i2} = proportion of workers in occupational status *i* with educational level 2.

We first cross-tabulate educational level by occupational status achieved (using the Hope-Goldthorpe scale). The results of this are given in Appendix Tables A4.1 to A4.4. One then subtracts the proportion of respondents with educational level 1 in occupational status *i* from the equivalent proportion from educational level 2 in the same occupational status. Secondly, all these differences in proportions are summed up over all occupational categories, ignoring signs, and the sum is divided by two. The index can take a value from a minimum of 0 (where both educational categories have exactly the same proportions in each occupational category) to a maximum of 1.0, where all of educational level 1 are in one set of occupational categories and all of educational level 2 are in another set of occupational categories (Duncan and Duncan, 1955; Tzanatos, 1990). The index, therefore, measures "how far" from complete segregation the two occupational distributions are. The larger the value, the greater the degree of dissimilarity. Table 4.1 gives these figures for all relevant contrasting sets of educational variables.

Table 4.1: The Degree of Dissimilarity (Duncan's "D") in the Occupational Distribution of Different Educational Levels (see Appendix Tables A4.1 to A4.3 for distributions)

Contrasting Educational Levels	First Job	First Permanent Job	Current Job
1. "D" between No Qualifications and Junior Cycle Qualifications	.16	.22	.29
2. "D" between Junior Cycle Qualifications and Leaving Certificate Qualifications	.32	.36	.40
3. "D" between Leaving Certificate Qualifications and RTC Certificate Qualifications	.26	.35	.37
4. "D" between RTC Certificate Qualifications and RTC Diploma Qualifications	.29	.35	.42
5. "D" between RTC Diploma Qualifications and University Degrees	.37	.40	.48

As can clearly be seen, the degree of dissimilarity increases with both educational level and time in the labour force. It is least pronounced — or most similar — amongst the least qualified, with only 16 per cent dissimilarity in the occupational distributions of those with "no qualifications" and those with junior cycle qualifications for first jobs. This increases — indeed almost doubles — over time to 29 per cent for current jobs. However, even after six years in the labour force, the degree of similarity in the occupational distributions of the least qualified is still very high, having the lowest degree of dissimilarity of all educational level contrasts. At the other extreme, the degree of dissimilarity is greatest between those with degrees and those with third level diploma qualifications. Starting off with over one-in-three being in clearly different occupational niches (assuming the same number of people in both educational categories), this increases to almost half by current job. This occurs at around three years in the labour market for those with diplomas and two years for those with degrees. So the extent of segregation increases significantly over time — primarily due, as we shall see later, to the more rapid upward career mobility of those with higher qualifications amongst those who first took up lower status occupations.

Contrasting the occupational distributions of third level graduates with those with lower level qualifications, the degree of similarity is greatest — or dissimilarity least — between those with a third level Certificate qualification and those with a Leaving Certificate; the dissimilarity index increasing from .26 to .37 from first job to current job.

There is very little overlap — or a high degree of dissimilarity — between those with a Leaving Certificate and those with degrees. For instance, for current job, "D" = .67, almost twice that of the CERT/ Leaving Certificate comparison. Furthermore, in the latter comparison the overlap is much greater amongst females than amongst males. So the greatest third level/second level overlap is between females with third level certificate and Leaving Certificate qualifications, particularly amongst those with business studies qualifications. This issue of the type of qualifications will be taken up later.

Three clear conclusions, therefore, appear justified:

- There is a significant degree of occupational differentiation between those entering the labour market with different levels of education — the higher the level of education, the better the occupation achieved.

- However, differently qualified, first-time job-seekers enter a wide range of occupations, particularly those with higher levels of qualification, with many of the latter taking up lower status occupations which significantly overlap with those who have second level qualifications only (see Appendix Table A4.2).

- Such overlaps, however, decline rapidly with time in the labour market, particularly for those with higher levels of qualification

— and particularly amongst those who initially entered lower status occupations. This aspect of upward career mobility will be explored in detail in the next section. However, even taking such upward mobility rates into account, and even after a number of years in the labour market, there is still substantial overlap in the occupational statuses achieved between those with neighbouring levels of education.

The Relationship between Educational Level and Occupational Status Achieved for First Jobs

The previous section reports on the overall degree of similarity or difference in the status of jobs entered by level of education. It shows that a substantial degree of overlap exists in occupations entered by people with different levels of education, particularly for first jobs. In this section, we describe in more detail the nature of that overlap by describing the changes in the median occupational status values, as well as the interquartile ranges, for each educational level in the three job categories: (a) "first job"; (b) first "permanent" job; and (c) current (1992) job. We choose the median rather than the average values, because they are less influenced by extreme values, but the average and standard deviation values are also given in Appendix Tables A4.2 to A4.5.

Comparing the three distributions over time, four clear patterns and trends are obvious. There is a very consistent and pronounced correlation between increasing educational levels and higher median (and average) occupational status levels, with the overall differences between educational levels increasing over time. There is a clear upward shift in the average occupational statuses of those with university degrees and, to an even greater extent, those with third level certificates/diplomas. The average scale values increase by eight to ten points for those with degrees and diplomas, compared to only three to five points for those with Leaving Certificate or lower qualifications, despite the fact that the former has been less than half the time of the latter in the labour market (see Appendix Table A4.5).

Table 4.2: Median, Inter-Quartile Range, Occupational Status Scale Values (Hope-Goldthorpe, 1974 Scale) for First Job, First Permanent Job and Current Job (for all labour market entrants, by level of education, 1992)

Job Progression	**Level of Education 1992**					
	No Quals	*JC*	*LC*	*Third Level Cert.*	*Third Level Dip.*	*Univ. Degree*
1. First Job						
Median Value	30	35	36	40	40	62
(Interquartile Range)	(9)	(10)	(12)	(20)	(36)	(30)
Total No.	91	366	756	111	72	184
2. First Permanent Job						
Median Value	33	35	37	40	53	62
(Interquartile Range)	(9)	(10)	(7)	(27)	(27)	(31)
Total No.	81	356	745	110	69	167
3. Current Job (If Employed)						
Median	35	36	40	51	62	62
(Interquartile Range)	(9)	(10)	(5)	(23)	(23)	(9)
Total No.	43	258	662	98	63	152

There is very little change, therefore, in the average status of those with second level qualifications. Even this, however, significantly understates the poorer labour market chances of those with no or poor qualifications. Those who never got a job (over one-in-five of those with no qualifications), or those who are currently unemployed or withdrawn from the labour force, are not included. Over 50 per cent of those with no qualifications and over 30 per cent of those with junior cycle qualifications, for instance, who did get a first job are either currently unemployed or have withdrawn from the labour force. This compares to only 12 per cent of those with a Leaving Certificate who are in the labour market for the same amount of time.

Comparison of and changes in the distributions and variances in occupational status achieved by educational level are even more revealing (see also Appendix Table A4.4). While the interquartile (IQ) ranges (Table 4.2) or standard deviations (Table A4.4) of those with second level qualifications are at all times lower than amongst those with third level qualifications, and do not change much over time, the variances of those with degrees and diplomas decrease substantially from first job to current job. Since the averages and variances vary widely, the coefficient of variation (standard deviation divided by mean) is a better measure of the relative variance. This declines substantially over time for those with third level qualification, while hardly changing for those with second level qualifications (see Table A4.5).

As a result, by current job, the interquartile range and relative variance of those with degrees is significantly smaller than all other educational levels. The main underlying reason for this decline in relative variances, for those with degrees and diplomas particularly, is the marked upward shift in the occupational statuses of those originally in the lowest quartile of their occupational distributions. This is clearly illustrated in Table 4.2 and Appendix Tables A4.1 to A4.4. The value of the lower IQ range, for instance, for degree holders increases from 35 to 62 and for diplomas from 27 to 40.

These data clearly suggest that when third level educated people enter the labour market, they take a very wide range of jobs which clearly overlap those with lower qualification levels. There is significant competition, for instance, between third level graduates — particularly those with certificates/diplomas — and those with a Leaving Certificate. Indeed, for first job — whether temporary or permanent — there is very little difference in the occupational distributions at the median to lower interquartile range for both these groups. There are, however, much wider relative variances in achievement for those with certificates/diplomas, with little direct competition between these and Leaving Certificate respondents at the upper occupational levels (see Appendix Tables A4.2 to A4.4). Equally, those with Leaving Certificate qualifications enter a very competitive market with those immediately below them in qualifications. This "overlap" declines significantly over time, however; with Leaving Certificate respondents being more upwardly mobile out of low-skilled manual and service jobs. Certificate/diploma graduates are equally more upwardly mobile out of "Leaving Certificate jobs". Since there is significant movement into unemployment, or out of the labour market altogether, by those with poor or no qualifications, these differential increases in occupational status values understate the relative inequalities in upward mobility chances.

Increasing "level congruence" over time in the labour market is, therefore, due mainly to those with higher qualifications moving upwards out of lower status jobs. As a result, the correlation between an individual's level of education and occupational status level increases over time, from a correlation (Pearson) of .33 for first job to a value of .56 for "current job". The extent and nature of upward career mobility is described in the following section.

Career Mobility

The results show some significant differences in career mobility chances, even restricting consideration only to those currently employed. Downward mobility most characterises those with least qualifications, particularly those with "no qualifications", and is least

Table 4.3: Extent of Upward and Downward Career Mobility amongst School Leavers by Level of Education 1992 (Hope-Goldthorpe Scale)

Extent of Career Mobility: First Permanent Job to Current Job	**Level of Education 1992**						
	No Quals	*JC*	*LC*	*Cert*	*Dip*	*Deg*	*Total*
	Per Cent						
Panel I							
Upward	28	32	29	27	31	10	27
Stable	44	52	60	62	59	83	61
Down	29	17	11	11	11	6	12
Total (%)	*100*	*100*	*100*	*100*	*100*	*100*	*100*
N	*42*	*256*	*657*	*97*	*61*	*145*	*1259*
	$x^2 = 139.7; df = 10; p<.001$						
Panel II							
Percentage of Total Sample Not Currently Employed and Not in Full-time Education	62	31	12	8	12	9	19
Total N	*115*	*378*	*763*	*114*	*75*	*215*	*1659*

characteristic of those with degrees. Given the marked upward mobility that occurs from "first job" to first permanent job, particularly for those with third level qualifications, they experience substantial status stability or upward mobility, particularly given their much shorter time in the labour force.

The bottom panel of Table 4.3 gives the percentage of respondents who are not employed and not in full-time education. Almost all of these are unemployed or have withdrawn from the labour force, mostly into "home duties". The results show a very pronounced relationship between low levels of education and unemployment/ withdrawal, with almost two-thirds of those not possessing any qualifications and almost a third of those with Junior Certificate qualifications in such non-employed statuses. So, unemployment, withdrawal or downward mobility is most characteristic of the least well qualified.

This pattern of differential mobility is clearly illustrated in Table 4.4, where we make a distinction between those who initially got their first permanent job in lower manual and service occupations (a status lower than most clerical workers (Hope-Goldthorpe scale point 40 — see Appendix Table A4.1)). This distinction does not exactly correspond with the manual/non-manual division in most

Table 4.4: Extent of Mobility from First Permanent Job to Current Job (by level of education (1992) and occupational status of first job)

Level of Education 1992	First Job in Non-Manual, Supervisory, Technical and Managerial/Professional Occupations (i.e., Hope-Goldthorpe ≥ 40)				First Job in Manual and Lower Service Occupations (<40 Hope-Goldthorpe Scale)			
	Career Mobility Job 1 → Current Job				*Career Mobility Job 1 → Current Job*			
	Upward	*Stable*	*Down*	*N*	*Upward*	*Stable*	*Down*	*N*
	Per Cent				*Per Cent*			
1. No Quals and JC Qualifications	0	73	27	(37)	35	48	17	(261)
2. LC Qualifications	7	81	12	(303)	48	42	10	(354)
3. Cert./Dip/ Degree	8	83	9	(234)	60	33	7	(70)

social mobility studies, but is close to it. Because of a "small number problem", we aggregate no qualifications with Junior Certificate qualifications, and degrees with certificates/diplomas.

Five clear patterns are evident:

- Of the limited number of respondents with less than Leaving Certificate qualifications who are still employed and who first entered non-manual occupations (N = 37), one-in-four are downwardly mobile — mostly into manual/service occupations. The rest are stable — mostly in manual/service supervisory positions. Of the great majority of those with junior cycle qualifications who entered middle to lower status manual/service occupations, on the other hand, there is also some downward mobility, though 35 per cent are upwardly mobile — mostly within the original manual/service category of occupations. The great majority of both, therefore, hold a stable position or are downwardly mobile. Even this considerably understates their undesirable position, however, with almost half either unemployed or withdrawn from the labour force altogether.

- The contrast with Leaving Certificate respondents is quite marked. Of the 44 per cent of Leaving Certificate respondents who first entered non-manual, supervisory and lower technical occupations, very few (12 per cent) are downwardly mobile. Most are stable, with some upward mobility. Of the remainder who initially entered manual/service occupations, almost half are upwardly mobile — mostly into lower non-manual occupations, with very little (ten per cent) downward mobility. In addition, those with a Leaving Certificate are much less likely to be unemployed or to have withdrawn from the labour force — only 12 per cent by 1992 (see Table 4.3).

- Almost all certificate/diploma and degree graduates who entered non-manual occupations are stable or upwardly mobile, with little downward mobility. Of the minority (26 per cent) who initially entered manual/service occupations, almost two-thirds are upwardly mobile — mostly into non-manual occupations. Very few are downwardly mobile. Taking lower status manual/service jobs appears to be a temporary phenomenon for most such graduates.

- Examining both sub-panels of the table, it is clear, firstly, that the probability of first entering manual/service occupations is highly correlated with educational level; and secondly, that the probability of staying on in such lower status positions is equally dependent on educational level. For those first entering manual/service occupations, the higher the level of education, the greater the level of upward mobility. For all groups, the lower the level of education, the higher the rate of downward mobility.
- A significant minority of third level graduates (particularly those with RTC certificates and diplomas), therefore, do take up jobs well "below" those which their level of educational status would warrant, but a majority of these are subsequently upwardly mobile. First jobs, therefore, even first "permanent" jobs, do not appear to be good indicators of even medium-term labour market outcomes, particularly for third level graduates.

The results also indicate a substantial amount of current unemployment and withdrawal from the labour force, particularly for those with no or poor educational qualifications who first take up low status manual/service occupations. Given this, and the general pattern of upward career mobility for the majority of Leaving Certificate and higher graduates who first took up manual/service occupations, it appears that there is a substantial reservoir of lower status and lower-paid manual/service jobs that are constantly being circulated or "swapped" amongst recent young entrants to the labour force — a substantial proportion of whom have rather high levels of education.

The Extent of Overqualification in the First Period in the Labour Market

The measure of "overqualification" used is described in detail in Chapter 2. This is a conservative measure of the extent to which school leavers with educational level X (for instance, those with a third level certificate) have occupational statuses more characteristic of those in the lower half[1] of the occupational distribution of those with an X–1 qualification (those with a Leaving Certificate). We

[1] At or below the median.

summarise the rates of overqualification by level of respondents' education in Table 4.5 (see Appendix Tables A4.1 to A4.3 for relevant occupational distributions).

Table 4.5: Extent of "Overqualification" in First Job, First Permanent Job and Current Job between Levels of Educational Achievement

Level of Education	**Percentage Overqualified**		
	First Job	*First Permanent Job*	*Current Job*
Leaving Certificate	47	39	26
Third Level Certificate	40	31	18
Third Level Diploma	57	42	27
University Degree	43	29	21

A comparison of the overqualification rates between those with third level qualifications and lower shows few systematic differences, with rates being over 40 per cent for all educational levels for first jobs, declining to just over 20 per cent for current jobs. The relative decline in this rate is much greater for those with third level qualifications, given that they have on average spent less than half the time of others in the labour market. There is a slightly greater tendency at all times for those with diplomas to have higher overlap than others — not perhaps unexpectedly, given the continuity in programmes of study and progression between certificate and diploma programmes in most regional technical colleges.

As already described, substantial upward career mobility occurs — particularly for those with third level education — over their first years in the labour market. Even after six years at work, however, over one-in-four Leaving Certificate respondents are in jobs for which they are clearly "overqualified", with around one-in-five third level graduates being equally disadvantaged. However, these results do not take into account examination grades. Previous research (Breen *et al.*, 1995) has shown that those with poor Leaving Certificate grades do no better in the labour market than those with reasonable Junior Certificate grades. So part of the reason for being assigned to and remaining stuck at the bottom of the occupational status scale by those with Leaving Certificate and higher qualifications may well be their poor examination achievements. In general, however, this would not hold for most third level graduates entering lower status occupational niches; but they, as we have seen, generally move rapidly upwards out of such niches within their first few years at work.

The Meaning of "Overeducation"

What meanings do respondents attach to our "overqualification" threshold? A number of subjective measures of overqualification have been used in the research literature, a variant of which we applied in our own study. We can use it to check whether respondents attach any substantive meaning to the thresholds chosen. A number of recent American and European studies of "overqualification" use respondents' own subjective assessments of the extent to which their own educational level, or type, was either "required" to get the job or to carry out the job effectively; or, as in the Hartog and Oosterbecks (1988) study, the extent to which their education was "the best preparation for the work you are carrying out". In our own study, we have a number of such measures, most of them closer to the earlier American PSID study (Duncan and Hoffman, 1981). This asks respondents in particular jobs the level of formal education required to get the job. If their own education is above that level, they are regarded as "overqualified". In all of these studies, however, jobs refer to those individually held by respondents, and analyses generally pay little attention to the structural characteristics of these jobs — particularly their occupational statuses.

We asked respondents who were ever employed the following two-part question:

"For your first job, what importance do you think your employer attached to the following things in your getting the job?

a) Your educational certificates and qualifications (e.g., Intermediate or Leaving Certificate, etc.); and

b) How well you did in your last examination (i.e., pass, honours, etc.)."

Responses were pre-coded from "a lot of importance" (= 3) to "not important" (= 1).

In the following table, we give respondents' views of the importance of their qualifications for those who are above and below the previously described (Chapter 2) "overqualification" threshold.

Table 4.6: Percentage of "Matched" and "Overqualified" Respondents who Said Education was Very Important in Getting Jobs, by Level of Education

Education Level Required to Get Job	**Level of Education**				
	No Quals	*Junior Cert.*	*Leaving Cert.*	*Third Level Cert./Dip*	*Univ. Degree*
	% "A Lot of Importance"				
1. Importance of Educational Qualifications:					
(a) Respondents Above Threshold ("Matched")	1	8	35	49	58
(b) Respondents Below Threshold ("Overqualified")	–	–	11	27	33
	% "A Lot of Importance"				
2. Importance of Examination Grades:					
(a) Respondents above Threshold ("Matched")	0	7	29	31	48
(b) Respondents below Threshold ("Overqualified")	–	–	11	14	20

Both Leaving Certificate and third level respondents who are "overqualified" for their jobs are substantially less likely to regard their educational credentials or their examination grades as being very important in getting their jobs than those who are "matched" to their jobs. These differences are greater for grades, with those "matched" to their jobs being two to three times more likely than the "overqualified" to regard their grades as being very important. For those with a Leaving Certificate, these differences in the perceived importance of educational qualifications and grades appear more clear-cut, with those "matched" to their jobs being around three times more likely to regard both as very important in getting their jobs. For those with third level qualifications, the relevant ratios are nearer 2:1. Two other aspects of these figures are relevant: the perceived "importance" of educational qualifications and examination grades increases substantially with level of education, as well as with occupational status achieved. Almost none of those with less than a Leaving Certificate thought qualifications/grade were very important, whereas over half of university graduates thought them very important.

Despite these patterns, however, over one-in-four of third level graduates taking up "second level jobs" (who are "overqualified") do think that their qualifications were very important in getting these low-level jobs, with between 14 and 20 per cent thinking examination grades were very important. It appears that many employers of unskilled and semi-skilled manual and service workers use qualifications in selecting "off the top" in making such appointments. They appear to have no difficulty in employing such "overqualified" labour, at least on a temporary basis.

The inter-correlations between respondents' perceptions of the importance of educational qualifications for employment and their educational level, as well as the status of the first and current occupations achieved, are reported in Table 4.7. The results mainly show:

(i) That there is a pronounced correlation between educational level achieved and occupational status achieved, with the importance increasing from first (temporary) to first "permanent" job, to current job;

(ii) That the extent to which educational qualifications are considered to be "important" increases both with level of education and with level of occupational status achieved;

(iii) That the status of "first job" and particularly "first permanent job" is highly correlated with the status of current (1992) job.

In other words, educational/occupational "level congruence" increases from first to current job; the perception of the importance of education increases also, at least up to the first permanent job; and both educational level and first occupational status are highly predictive of subsequent occupational statuses achieved.

Table 4.7: Pearson Correlations between Level of Education, Occupational Statuses Achieved and Perceived Employer Reliance on Educational Qualifications in Job Decisions (3 = A Lot of Importance → 1 = No Importance)

	1	2	3	4	5
	Final Educational Level	*Occ. Status "First Job"*	*Occ. Status of First Permanent Job*	*Occ. Status Final/ Current Job*	*Importance of Educational Qualifications*
1. Final Educational Level Achieved	1.00				
2. Occupational Status — First Job	.46	1.00			
3. Occupational Status — First "Permanent" Job	.54	.84	1.00		
4. Occupational Status — Job at 1992 Interview	.56	.59	.70	1.00	
5. Extent to Which Respondent Felt that Educational Qualifications were Important in Getting First Job	.40	.35	.39	.37	1.00

The great majority of the more poorly qualified, however, do not think that educational "level" or "grades" achieved are as important as they appear to be (see Table 4.6). Given that the chances of getting a job, and particularly a good job, are actually moderately too highly correlated with educational level achieved, as well as grades achieved in examinations — even in Junior Certificate examinations (Breen *et al.*, 1995) — their perception of their relative unimportance is puzzling. This lack of perceived rewards for good examination results, or for staying on to complete the Leaving Certificate, amongst those with such poor schooling outcomes, is obviously a strongly negative contributory factor to their lack of educational success.

In order to check whether the increasing correlation between level of education and occupational status with time in the labour market also holds for older ages, we show in Table 4.8 the correlations between current occupational status (using the Irish Census, six-value, "social class" scale) and educational level for four age groups, from the 1996 Labour Force Survey (Micro-Data Set, Public Use Sample).

Table 4.8: Correlation between Level of Education and Occupational Status** of Current Job (for employed respondents, various age groups)*

	Age 20–24	**Age 25–29**	**Age 30–34**	**Age 35–39**
Correlation (Pearson) Between Educational Level and Occupational Status of Current Job	r = .47	r = .56	r = .54	r = .57
Total N	*6391*	*6797*	*6959*	*6887*

Source: Micro Data Set, Public Use Sample, Labour Force Survey, 1996.

Notes: * Level of education has six values: 1 = No formal education or Primary Education; 2 = Intermediate/Group; 3 = Leaving Cert.; 4 = Third level non-University; 5 = Third level University; 6 = Higher University Degree.

** "Social Class" (occupational status) has six values: 6 = Higher Professional/ Managerial; 5 = Lower Professional/Managerial; 4 = Intermediate Non-Manual; 3 = Skilled Manual; 2 = Semiskilled Manual; 1 = Unskilled Manual. Farmers are distributed according to size of farm.

The results indicate clearly that correlations increase significantly between ages 20–24 and older groups, though not amongst those older than 30. Since most third level graduates would have entered the labour market by age 23–24, the full range of educational levels is represented in the 20–24 age group — though obviously not as many third level graduates as in the 25–29 age group. The correlations are remarkably similar to those in our sample results in Table 4.7. These results strongly indicate that "level congruence" does increase with age and time in the labour force — but only up to the 25–29 age group. It appears to be only in the first "settling down" period in the labour market, therefore, that the relationship between "educational level" and "occupational level" improves. In the initial, "first jobs", stage, it appears that many highly educated school/college leavers take lower status jobs, but as they age, a significant proportion of such "overqualified" young workers move up to better and more "level congruent" jobs, with "level congruence" increasing as the "settling down" occurs.

SUMMARY

This chapter reports the results of a number of measures of similarity in the occupations first entered by school/college leavers from different levels of education. It also summarises information on the average and median values and distributions, of occupations taken by differently qualified leavers; also describing the extent and nature of occupational mobility from first to current job.

The two measures of occupational similarity/dissimilarity and overqualification used tell much the same story: that as young people enter work from different educational levels, there is initially a substantial degree of overlap in occupations taken up. Indeed, for first jobs, high similarity in occupational distributions is almost the norm. However, with increasing time in the labour market, a moderate to high degree of occupational segregation between those with neighbouring levels of education emerges. Even after only two years in the labour market, third level graduates, particularly those with degrees, move rapidly upwards out of even skilled manual/ technical and lower non-manual jobs — occupations dominated by those with Leaving Certificate and lower qualifications (see Appendix Tables A4.2 to A4.4.) However, even after a number of years at work, around one-in-five of those with degrees are still in jobs more characteristic of those with a Leaving Certificate — for example, at clerical or intermediate non-manual level or lower. It may well be, of course, that such graduates have unmeasured and unrewarding educational and personal attributes which would have prevented them from attaining even that level of occupational status had their education been poorer.

Getting any job at all and then holding on to it is a major achievement for those without any qualifications, or with poor junior cycle ones, with almost two-thirds of the former and one-third of the latter without current (1992) employment. Not only are they less likely to be upwardly mobile from first job, but they are also far more likely to be excluded permanently from the work force. A good educational qualification is a necessary personal resource, with people without such being increasingly and cumulatively excluded from effective participation in the economy and society.

An important dimension of that exclusionary process is the apparently growing extent to which better-educated young people, particularly those with third level qualifications, now take up lower-skilled service occupations — particularly in the retail, restaurant and bar trades — on a part-time basis while in college and on a temporary basis on graduation, while they wait around to get a "real" job. Most of these occupations were previously the preserve of those with lower levels of education. Indeed, many of these jobs originally required apprenticeship training, such as bar tender, waiter and shop assistant. However, as youth unemployment rates and educational levels grew from the early 1980s onwards, even as many of these low-skilled service jobs rapidly expanded, employers gradually came to "pick off the top" of the queue of job applicants; and also gradually transformed a significant proportion of these jobs into part-time and temporary ones. The extent and nature of that transformation requires a more detailed study, but the effects are clearly discernible: employment exclusion at the bottom of the educational ladder and a significant element of initial and (mostly) temporary movement into low-status jobs at the top. Of course, as labour demand increases and supply declines from the late 1990s onwards, these employment strategies will become non-viable, with these initially high levels of "overqualification" amongst the better educated being likely to decline rapidly.

Chapter 5

Returns to Level of Education: Occupational Achievement and Earnings

As already described, there is a moderate to high correlation between educational level achieved and status of first jobs in Ireland, though a substantial proportion of the more highly educated do start off in low status jobs. In this chapter, we estimate these relationships using multivariate regression methods. Because many factors other than educational level affect employment chances and occupational status achieved — like gender and social class of origin (Breen, 1995) — we need to control for such extraneous effects and specify a more general model of occupational status achievement.

We test five main hypotheses:

- Level of education achieved is expected to have the greatest effect on occupational status of first job; but both of these are themselves hypothesised to have the main effects, independently and additively, on subsequent career opportunities.
- Controlling for the effects of level of education and initial occupational status achieved, however, it is hypothesised that the more highly educated who are "overqualified" for first jobs are less likely to be upwardly mobile than the "level matched"; that there is a negative "threshold effect" below which low-status jobs disproportionately hurt subsequent career chances.
- Specialisation in vocational-technical subjects at second level, or professional/technical qualifications at third level, are both expected to increase the probability of "level matching" in first and current jobs; and both are expected to increase the rate of upward career mobility from first to current job.

- Earnings are hypothesised to be affected by two main variables: level of education achieved and occupational status achieved, with both expected to have independent and additive effects.
- "Overqualified" workers, however, are hypothesised to have higher earnings than "level matched" workers — with additional returns to additional human capital within specific occupational categories. "Underqualified", workers, on the other hand, are expected to have lower earnings for the opposite reason.

We first estimate the independent and additive effects of social background and educational achievement on first job status. Second, we estimate the relative effects of both sets of variables on subsequent career mobility and current occupational status, specifically testing for the effects of "overqualification" on subsequent career chances. Finally, we examine the relationship between educational and occupational status achievement variables and earnings.

MULTIVARIATE ANALYSIS OF FACTORS AFFECTING OCCUPATIONAL STATUS ACHIEVED: FIRST JOB TO CURRENT JOB

We start by using the original individual occupational status attainment model (Blau and Duncan, 1967; Duncan *et al.*, 1972; Sewell and Hauser, 1975). In this model, current occupational status attained is dependent on an individual's social origins (parental SES and education, her/his level of academic ability, and a set of educational achievement and work experience variables which both mediate social background variables, and act independently to affect occupational status achievement). In the next chapter we will examine the effects of some structured labour market variables, particularly industrial/occupational segment entered. The following simple model is the classic Blau and Duncan (1967) path diagram.

Figure 5.1: Path Diagram of Occupational Achievement Model

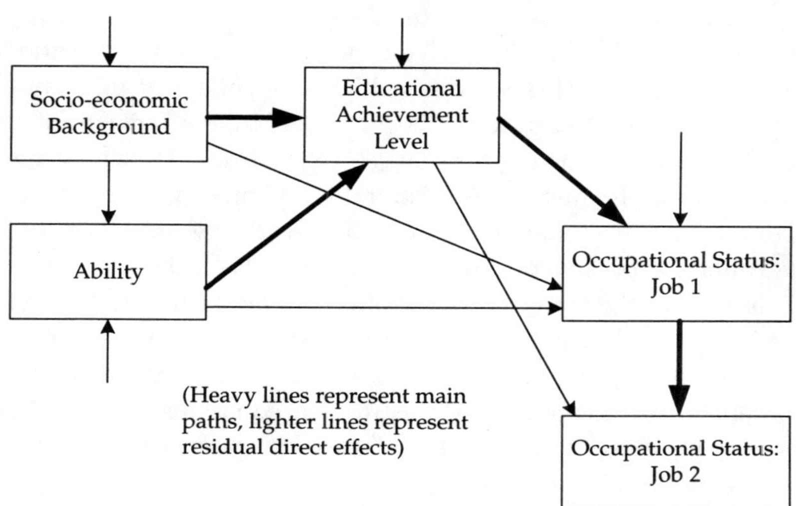

Socio-economic status of origin (SES) and individual ability mainly and directly affect educational achievement. Although most of the effects of these background variables are mediated through educational achievement, the three variables jointly affect initial occupational attainment. In regression terms, SES of origin and ability combined explain almost 60 per cent of the variance in educational achievement in Ireland (Hannan *et al.*, 1996) and, combined with educational level, around 40 per cent of the variance in occupational status attainment in American studies, though education explains most of it (see Sewell and Hauser, 1975: 51).

In the following table, we set out our own somewhat more elaborated model of the variables likely to affect both educational achievement (see Hannan, *et al.*, 1996) and occupational status achieved. Our main objective is to assess the extent to which educational level explains occupational status achievement and mediates the effects of social background factors. As Breen's (1995, 1997) analyses indicate it would appear that social background (particularly social class) factors retain greater significance in the Irish case. In column 1, Table 5.1, the combined set of family background variables — which index both the class (economic)[1] and socio-cultural (the "cultural capital")[2] aspects of family background with gender — explains 20 per cent of the variance in educational achievement levels. This is quite a high percentage of educational achievement explained in terms of purely "objective" structural and cultural factors — showing how structured educational achievement chances are in Ireland. It is also rather similar to the variance explained in examination grade achieved by similar social background factors in a recent study (Hannan *et al.*, 1996).

Column 2 of the table shows the effects of all these variables, plus educational level achieved, on the occupational status of first permanent job. By comparing the regression coefficients for each set of variables in these successive regression equations, we can both determine the extent to which "prior" variables persist in their effects on occupational status achieved and the extent to which they are mediated through educational level. In this case, it is very clear that, although educational level is by far the most important variable in explaining the occupational status level of first job, gender, mother's educational level and region still retain significance.

Almost all other variable effects which were significant for educational level have become insignificant — or are almost fully mediated by educational level. This result contrasts with that of Breen (1995), who finds a significant influence of father's occupational status on children's occupational achievement levels (though he did not include mother's educational level in his regression, and his study dealt only with second level leavers). It appears from this result that, although the socio-economic background effects are almost fully mediated by educational level achieved, background socio-cultural influences still persist in occupational status achievement. It appears that the positive effects of socialisation in personal and interpersonal characteristics which occur in families where mothers are better educated have persistent

---

1 Socio-economic resources are indexed by father's unemployment status, his occupational status and number of children.

2 "Cultural Capital" is indexed both by mother's education and west of Ireland origins (West = 1; Else = 0). See Hannan *et al.* (1996).

Table 5.1: Effects of Socio-economic and Socio-cultural Background on Educational Achievement; and with the Latter on Occupational Achievement (Multiple Regression (OLS) method)

Independent Variables	**Equation 1**	**Equation 2**	**Equation 3**	**Equation 4**
	Educational Level Achieved	*Occupational Status of First Perm. Job*	*Current Occupational Status (i)*	*Current Occupational Status (ii)*
A. Social Background Variables	β	β	β	β
1. Father's Occupational Status	−.02**	−.06	−.04	−.04
2. Father Unemployed: (1 = Unemployed; 0 = Other)	−.26**	.47	.46	.30
3. Mother's Educational Level	.32**	1.51**	.68*	.66*
4. Number of Children in Family	−.04*	−.15	.14	.11
5. Gender (1 = F; 0 = M)	.26**	1.99**	−1.1*	−1.0*
6. Region of Origin (1 = West; 0 = Else)	.30**	−1.46*	−.87	−.81
B. Respondent's Educational Level				
7. Level of Educational Achievement	–	5.48**	2.64**	1.73**
C. Occupational Status Achieved and Employment Experience				
8. Occupational Status of First Permanent Job	–	–	.56**	.65**
9. "Overeducated" for First Permanent Job	–	–	–	4.31**
10. Local Non-Dublin	–	–	–	−1.33*
11. Emigrant	–	–	–	.25
R^2 =	.20	.32	.54	.55
df =	6/1143	7/1142	8/1141	11/1138
p =	< .001	<.001	< .001	< .001

** $p < .01$; * $p < .05$.

Note: Size of firm, promotion within current job, time in labour market or in current job have non-significant effects on current occupational status.

— though modest — influences on occupational chances, at least for the initial period in the labour force.[3] Gender has a clear positive effect — mostly due to the high concentration of females in clerical occupations, with males being more concentrated in manual (including skilled manual) occupations. Interestingly, region of origin continues to have effects. However, this is almost entirely due to those from western/rural regions who remain at home and suffer occupationally for so doing.

In column 3 of the table (equation 3), we report the regression results for current occupational status, using the occupational status of first job and all the preceding variables as explanatory variables. Although occupational status of first job is the main explanatory variable, both educational level and maternal education retain significant influence (as they did for first job), although both effects are substantially reduced. So, although most of the effects are mediated by occupational status of first job, respondents' education retains substantial independent effects. Increasing educational levels continue to have positive independent effects on career chances — irrespective of the status of first (permanent) job achieved. This finding of the continual relevance of education to promotion chances (within firms), and in upward career mobility generally, supports earlier work in the United States (Spilerman, 1986) as well as other recent work in Ireland (Breen and Whelan, 1998). It suggests that such educational credential differences measure real human capital differences, not mere "signals" used initially to select amongst people in labour market queues.

Controlling for educational level and gender (female=1, male=0) has an additional positive effect on first job; though being female has a consistent negative — though smaller — effect on subsequent mobility chances (see equations 3 and 4).

We add in "overeducation" and other labour market variables in equation 4. They add slightly to the explained variance and two of the findings are of particular importance. Taking up a first job for

---

[3] It may, of course, be due to the fact that many educated mothers are more likely to work and be employed in high status and better paid jobs. Previous work (Hannan *et al.*, 1996) showed that, although maternal employment and occupational status has some limited positive impact on children's educational achievement, maternal education has much clearer effects.

which one was "overeducated" clearly does not have any additional negative effect on subsequent occupational achievement, once occupational status of first job is controlled for. There appears, therefore, to be no additional occupational status boundary below which the highly educated are disproportionately disadvantaged; i.e., once occupational status of first job is controlled for. Indeed, the positive coefficient for "overeducation" suggests that when the more highly educated initially take up disproportionately low status jobs they subsequently more than proportionally move upwards out of them. The hypothesis of a negative "threshold effect" for "overqualification" is, therefore, strongly rejected. Indeed, given the large positive effect, it appears as if the very low status jobs taken by those (mainly) third-level-educated leavers have not been considered as "real" jobs by subsequent employers. They appear to be "too low" to be considered as validly measuring the potential real productivity of employees. On the other hand, those in first occupations just above the threshold appear to pay a price for such low levels of "acceptable" achievements; i.e., within the wide range of occupations that third level graduates are broadly expected to enter.

Besides educational level and occupational status of first job, a number of other labour market experience variables were not significant: for example, size of firm and length of time in labour force. So, at least as measured in the first few years in the labour market, the extent of work experience is not substitutable for educational achievement, an effect that has been supported in some American studies (Sicherman, 1991). However, compared to those who migrate, respondents who stay on in their local, non-metropolitan counties of origin clearly pay a price — in lower occupational achievement — for so doing. Obviously, both constraints on moving away from the home community and compensating non-economic advantages in staying locally need to be significant to counterbalance such clear occupational disadvantages (see Sexton *et al.*, 1991).

The Effect of Vocational/Technical and Professional Qualifications

The hypothesis that vocational/technical qualifications at second level, or professional/technical qualifications at third level, increase the probability of getting "level matched" jobs and decrease that of taking up jobs for which one was "overqualified", is not supported by the evidence from this survey — at least for first job and first permanent job (see Appendix Tables A5.1 to A5.3). In fact, those who took one or more vocational/technical subjects in their second level examinations (like woodwork, metalwork and technical drawing, etc.) were slightly more likely to be overqualified for their first jobs. Those with professional/technical qualifications at third level (engineering, applied science, medicine, etc.) have roughly the same rate of "overqualification" as those without such specialisations. So, in each case the hypothesis is not supported.

This is not the case, however, for current occupations. Those with professional/technical qualification at third level have a clear advantage in reduced "overqualification" levels. Obviously, such qualifications are a significant help in seeking upward mobility out of first jobs. This is not the case, however, for those with second level vocational/technical subject specialisations. These are, in fact, less likely than others to be upwardly mobile out of lower status jobs — suggesting that such qualifications also indicate lower examination achievements (see Hannan and Ó Riain, 1993).

The addition of these two independent education variables to multiple regression equations predicting current occupational status strongly supports the above conclusions (see Appendix Table A5.3). Taking vocational/technical subjects is negatively related to current occupational achievement levels, controlling for level of education, original occupational status achieved and other confounding variables. Such types of qualification, however, do appear to increase the probability of employment and of subsequently securing access to more skilled employment — or of escaping unskilled and insecure employment (see Hannan and Ó Riain, 1993; Shavit and Müller, 1998). On the other hand, having professional/technical qualifications subsequently increases upward career mobility chances, irrespective of first job status and other confounding variables. Essentially, therefore, neither type of qualification protects from low status of first job, but professional/technical qualifications significantly improve subsequent upward career mobility chances; and while vocational/technical qualifications do not improve upward career mobility — apparently setting a boundary to upward movement at skilled manual levels — they do appear to help escape from low-skilled and insecure employment.

In conclusion, two of the three relevant hypotheses are supported. Level of education is the main variable predicting initial occupational achievement, though socio-cultural status of origin retains important independent effects. Though initial occupational status achieved is the main variable predicting subsequent occupational achievement, educational level does retain substantial continuing influence (see also Breen and Whelan, 1998). In addition, professional/technical qualifications do reduce "overqualification" rates for current jobs, and do increase the rate of upward career mobility.

However, other hypotheses are rejected. Once educational level and occupational status of first job are controlled for, being "overqualified" for first job does not have additional negative, threshold effects on upward mobility chances. Indeed, it is almost as if some compensating positive effect occurs — as if most of those with third level qualifications who take such low status jobs are disproportionately upwardly mobile. However, as we have seen in Chapter 4, a significant minority of these do remain trapped in such jobs. The hypothesis of specific negative threshold effects is, however, strongly rejected. However, specialisation in vocational-technical subjects at second level actually reduces opportunities for upward mobility.

EARNINGS

Our main concern in this section is to measure the influence that educational level and occupational status achieved have on earnings, as well as whether "surplus education" (or "overeducation") has the effect hypothesised, i.e., whether, controlling for level of education and all other relevant educational, occupational and work experience variables, "overqualification" actually receives higher levels of remuneration as the literature suggests. We start with the variables that were significant in the final regression equation in Table 5.1, and test to see to what extent these variables — and being "undereducated" or "overeducated" for one's occupation — have significant additional effects on earnings.

The results of the regression (Table 5.2) are somewhat equivalent to the original American figures (Sewell and Hauser, 1975), though with somewhat more clear-cut results about the effects of level of education. The combined set of independent variables explains 32 per cent of the variance in gross hourly earnings (the most relevant earnings variable).

Table 5.2: Effects of Social Background, Gender, Educational Level, Occupational Status, Work Experience and "Overqualification" on Earnings (gross per hour, for current job, Irish-based workers,[†] OLS regression)

Independent Variables	**Equation 1**	**Equation 2**	**Equation 3**	**Equation 4**
	Log Earnings per Hour (Gross)			
A. Socio-economic & Socio-Cultural Background Variables	β	β	β	β
1. Father's Occupational Status	.003*	.003	.003*	.003
2. Mother's Educational Level	.02	.02	.02	.02
3. Gender: (1=Female; 0=Male)	–.07*	–.09**	–.08**	–.10**
4. Level of Education Achieved	.08**	.09**	.07**	.08*
B. Occupational Achievement and Labour Market Variables				
5. Occupational Status Achieved	.01**	.01*	.01**	.01*
6. Amount of Time Employed	.001	.001	.001	.001
7. Number of Jobs	–.003	–.004	–.001	.01
8. Size of Firm	.07**	.08**	.07**	.07**
9. Labour Market Locality				
(a) Local Dublin	–.02	–.03	–.02	–.03
(b) Local Non-Dublin	–.10**	–.11**	–.10**	–.11*
C. "Overqualification" Variables				
10. "Overqualified" for Job		–.24**	–	–.23**
11. "Underqualified" for Job		–.07	–	–.07
12. Belief that Educational Level and Grades Achieved were Important in Getting Job		–	.03	.02
$R^2 =$	*0.32*	*0.34*	*0.32*	*0.34*
df =	*10/651*	*12/649*	*11/650*	*13/648*
p =	*< .001*	*< .001*	*< .001*	*< .001*

** p< .01; * p< .05; [†] Information on gross earnings for emigrants is largely incomplete. Since the ratio of net to gross earnings varies so significantly by national tax takes, and we have few (N=30) cases where both types of income data are available, it is not possible to reliably estimate the net to gross ratios for emigrants.

In terms of explaining gross hourly earnings, two variables stand out as most important: occupational status achieved and level of education. More than half of the effects of education level are mediated through occupational status achieved, but both combined explain more of the variance than any other set of variables. In other words, within occupational categories, higher educational levels return higher earnings; employers reward such increased human capital attributes with more highly remunerated jobs. Initial human capital (in level of education achieved), therefore, not only has substantial effects on occupational status achieved but, when we control for the effects of the latter and other relevant variables, educational level still continues to have a significant positive effect on earnings. This result replicates the early American studies (Sewell and Hauser, 1975: 63–64).

Time in labour market and number of jobs have no additional effects.[4] Given the nature of the sample — with almost no variance on the former variable amongst those with second level qualifications — we would not have expected much of an effect. However, two other variables are important: size of firm and job location. Not unexpectedly, the larger the size of firm, the higher the earnings. Staying on in one's local county also has clear negative earnings effects. So, despite controlling for occupational status achieved — which is also negatively affected — such local loyalties have additional negative effects on earnings. There must be many compensatory advantages, therefore, to such non-migrant decisions and also substantial social constraints on migrating (Hannan, 1970).

Women, however, do not gain as much as men in earnings in current jobs. Since women appear to have a significant advantage in first job placements (Table 5.1), and a significant minority of the more poorly educated women have already withdrawn from the labour force, the wage gap has emerged quite early in their careers — a wage gap apparent in most Irish studies (see Callan and Wren, 1994).

In equation 2, we test for the additional earnings effect of being "overqualified" or "underqualified" (both dummy variables). All of the other relevant variables being controlled for, the effect of being

---

[4] Time in labour market is highly correlated with level of education, with third level College leavers having almost one-third of time in the labour market compared to non-College leavers.

"overqualified" for one's job is clearly negative for gross (and net) hourly and weekly earnings. So, contrary to our hypotheses and most international findings, the "overqualified" pay not only a significant social cost in lower occupational status achieved, but also a significant additional earnings cost in lower (gross and net) incomes within the lower-status occupational category achieved. So, within the set of lower-status occupational categories in which they remain concentrated (given that over half of those originally "overqualified" subsequently become upwardly mobile), the residual "overqualified" group are clearly not being rewarded by Irish employers for their greater marginal human capital. In fact, quite the reverse: it is almost as if employers under-rate, and consequently under-pay, the over-qualified who remain in these lower status occupations — or have been unable to get higher status jobs. There may of course be a substantial element of self-selection involved, with the more highly educated still remaining in low status jobs after a number of years in the labour market being characterised by other negative, unobserved attributes — hence the lower pay. Whatever the underlying reason for retention in these lower status jobs, however, the hypothesis of higher wage/salary returns for them is unambiguously rejected. In the overcrowded Irish youth labour market, the overqualification problem is not only present and costly to produce; it is also costly in its outcomes for the better-educated school/college leaver.

What about the "undereducated"? If we use a similar approach to the "overqualification" definition — i.e., those having an occupational status clearly higher than that of the median of the next higher level of education — we get much smaller numbers, but the effect is negative, though not statistically significant. This negative result conforms to that of the research literature.

The final two equations in Table 4.4 examine the effects of respondents' own assessments of how important their educational qualification and examination grades were in getting their first job (scores ranging from 4 = "a lot" of importance for both, to 0 = "no importance"). In equation 3, we show the additional effect of this assessment on its own. Such perceived education-by-job matching has no additional effect on its own in or in combination with the more objective "overqualification" measures. This non-predictive power of the subjective "overqualification" measure in both equations 3 and 4 is not only of importance in itself but also supportive of the validity of our approach in using objective measures. Whether or not respondents believe that their educational qualifications/grades were closely matched to their first jobs has no independent effect on current earnings levels.

SUMMARY

The finding that educational level achieved is significantly dependent on social origins, particularly social class and parental education, and that such family background effects continue on to first job chances, shows a high degree of class structuring of both educational chances and labour market opportunities in the Irish system (see also Breen, 1995; and Breen and Whelan, 1998).

The linkage between educational and occupational achievement are shown to be primarily vertical: the more the better, with only limited returns to type of education. Those results and those of the previous chapter show a significant association between educational level and occupational status achieved, and one that grows over the first few years in the labour market. Initial exclusion and the less direct gradual and cumulative exclusion from labour participation is primarily limited to those with the poorest levels of education.

Once educational and initial occupational variables are controlled for, being "overeducated" for first job, rather than having any additional negative effect on upward career mobility, appears to have had a slight positive "catching up" effect on subsequent career mobility. Gender, which had a slight positive effect on the status of first job, has a negative effect on subsequent career mobility chances.

Type of education — though having no consistent effect on first job status — does have a consistent and clear effect on subsequent career chances. Those specialising in (second level) vocational/technical subjects have lower overall rates of upward career mobility — though previous work shows an improvement in access to skilled manual work by such graduates (Hannan and Ó Riain, 1993). But this appears to ignore a "ceiling effect" on further upward mobility (see Shavit and Müller, 1998). On the other hand those with professional/technical qualifications (at third level) have clear advantages over their peers in achieving upward career mobility from first jobs.

Besides the highly significant educational and occupational status effects, the main findings of the earnings equations are that "overqualification" has a clear negative affect, once all other confounding variables are controlled for. This is contrary to most international research. It suggests that, for the minority of young people who still remain in occupations that are lower in status than their education would warrant, even after a number of years in the Irish labour market, their employers perceive them to have lower productivity levels than their colleagues in the same occupations who are "level matched", and hence pay them less. This productivity interpretation is given some credence by the corresponding finding that the "underqualified" (those in higher occupational statuses than their education would warrant) are also underpaid relative to their "level congruent" peers (though the effect is not statistically significant) — a finding which is in agreement with most international research in this area.

Chapter 6

Segmentation in the Youth Labour Market: "Overqualification" and Returns to Education

INTRODUCTION

In contrast to human capital theory (which focuses on the productivity-enhancing characteristics of individual workers' education and training characteristics in determining productivity, earnings, etc.) labour market segmentation theory emphasises the characteristics of jobs and firms and the way they are organised and located within different sectors of the economy. Original dual labour market theory divided the labour market into two segments: (i) a primary sector, with good, well-paying jobs, good working conditions and promotion prospects and high returns to education (though these jobs are rationed and persons are both recruited and promoted on the basis of their educational quality); and (ii) the secondary sector, where jobs are poor, with poor working conditions and promotion prospects, but also where mobility out of such sectors is severely constrained (Doeringer and Piore, 1971). Hence, job rewards and promotion prospects are hypothesised to depend as much on sector entered as on individuals' own human capital characteristics. Intrinsic to the model is the proposition that jobs in the primary sector are rationed, and that job allocation and promotion processes are determined to a greater extent by rational/technical (human capital) norms than in the secondary sector. So, it is proposed that significant barriers to entry from the secondary sector protect primary sector workers from competition and maintain their advantages: these advantages are not competed away (McNabb and Ryan, 1990). Because of severe conceptual and empirical critiques of this dual labour market model, it fell into disrepute, but has more recently been resuscitated by the specification of a more sophisticated "segmented labour market" model (see reviews by Hughes and Nolan, 1997; Dickens and Lang, 1985, 1993; Blackaby *et al.*, 1995).

Hughes and Nolan (1997) and Smyth (1997) developed and applied the theory to Irish data; the former focusing on the divergence between labour market segments in the way earnings are determined, and the latter the relationship between segmentation and gender differentiation in the labour market. The results of Hughes and Nolan's (1997) work showed significant differences in the rates of return to education between workers in the primary and secondary sectors — particularly between the latter and the primary professional/technical sector, where returns are significantly higher, though less so than in the United States.

Besides the literature on labour market segmentation, the research literature on the youth labour market has also criticised the working assumptions of the individualistically biased "occupational attainment" model, in implicitly accepting that the labour market is an open and relatively unconstrained, competitive one with few barriers to mobility. The work of Ashton and his colleagues using British data (Ashton *et al.*, 1990; 1992) shows that the initial "entry point" into the labour market (in occupational/industrial terms, whether semi-skilled and unskilled manual or service jobs, or lower non-manual or semi-professional/technical jobs) has a significant influence on subsequent employment security and occupational mobility, independently of personal characteristics or educational achievements (Ashton and Sung, 1992). As Spilerman's (1977) criticism of the status attainment model made clear, the changes in statuses and earnings from first to current job are, to some extent, "scheduled" by the labour market sector and "career line" (if any) present in the firms, industries and occupations originally taken up. Breen's (1984a, 1984b) work on the Irish youth labour market also showed that unemployment was more likely to occur where young people entered the secondary, exposed sector of the labour market. Ashton and his colleagues (Ashton *et al.*, 1990; Ashton and Sung, 1992) also showed that, in the British youth labour market at least, youth exclusion from "adult segments" had significant negative effects on subsequent unemployment, training and promotion.

Besides the effects of entering secondary labour market segments, the concentration of young workers (15–19; 20–24) in particular industrial segments has received considerable research attention. The recent OECD review of the issue (*Employment Outlook*, 1996b), for instance, showed a high degree of concentration in four industrial categories: retail and wholesale, hotels and restaurants, personal services, and construction (all "secondary" by most definitions), with over 40 per cent of all young workers concentrated in these sectors in many of the advanced industrial countries — the degree of concentration being two to three times greater than amongst adults.

This research on labour market segmentation and, in particular, the effects of labour market segment on youth employment opportunities and earnings, yields the following two hypotheses:

- Controlling for level of education and occupational status achieved, entering secondary labour market segments significantly increases the probability of subsequent unemployment and withdrawal from the labour force.
- School leavers entering the secondary labour market sector face significant additional barriers to upward occupational mobility, controlling for level of education achieved and occupational status of first job.

LABOUR MARKET SEGMENT AND CONCENTRATION OF YOUTH EMPLOYMENT

As we can see from Table 6.1, concentration in secondary sector jobs is very high amongst those leaving school before the Leaving Certificate and taking up their first jobs. Fifty-six per cent of pre-Leaving Certificate pupils are concentrated in "secondary" industrial sectors — retail/wholesale, personal services and construction — with agriculture/fishing adding another 11 per cent. Thus, over two-thirds of such early school leavers are concentrated in such industrial sectors.

For those with a Leaving Certificate, concentration is slightly less only in personal services and construction, with retail/wholesale, however, having comparable concentrations: 46 per cent in total being in these three segments, and another six per cent in agriculture. So, although high, this concentration is substantially less for those with a Leaving Certificate.

Table 6.1: Industry of First Job by Level of Education (School/College Leavers follow-up survey)

Industry	**Pre-Leaving Cert.**	**Leaving Cert.**	**Third Level**	**Total**
	%	%	%	%
1. Agriculture/Fishing	10.7	6.4	3.4	7.0
2. Manufacturing	25.1	17.6	17.5	19.7
3. Construction	10.3	5.9	7.7	7.6
4. Retail/Wholesale	23.9	25.3	13.6	22.2
5. Personal Services	22.1	15.1	11.9	16.4
6. Professional Services	3.0	13.5	26.9	13.6
7. Banking/Insurance	1.5	7.7	7.7	5.9
8. Others	3.5	8.3	11.2	7.9
Total %	*100*	*100*	*100*	*100*
N	*457*	*755*	*370*	*1582*

For those who went on to third level, initial concentration in these three sectors is considerably lower (33 per cent), with only three per cent in agriculture. On the other hand, jobs in professional services, banking, financial services and public administration account for over a third of graduates' first jobs — compared to only five per cent for those with less than a Leaving Certificate. Interestingly, manufacturing and construction employment is less biased across educational levels, though those with pre-Leaving Certificate qualifications are more likely to be in such jobs.

Whether secondary sector employment declines with experience in the labour force is analysed in Table 6.2. It shows a clear decline in retail/wholesale and personal service employment from first to current job. This decline from 46 to 43 to 30 per cent for pre-Leaving Certificate workers; from 40 to 39 to 29 per cent for Leaving Certificate workers; and from 26 to 18 to 15 per cent for third level graduates. So there is a clear-cut gradual movement out of secondary sectors of the economy for all educational levels, though the rate of decline is greatest for third level graduates.

Table 6.2: Industry of First Permanent Job and Current Job by Level of Education

Industry	Pre-Leaving Cert.		Leaving Cert.		Third Level		Total	
	First Permanent Job	*Current Job*	*First Permanent Job*	*Current Job*	*First Permanent Job*	*Current Job*	*First Permanent Job*	*Current Job*
1. Agriculture/ Fishing	9.5	8.5	6.0	5.1	3.1	2.3	6.4	5.2
2. Manufact.	27.0	30.0	18.3	23.4	20.7	23.7	21.3	25.0
3. Construction	10.2	16.0	6.0	5.6	6.6	4.5	7.4	7.8
4. Retail/ Wholesale	20.1	16.5	25.0	20.5	8.0	5.9	19.8	16.0
5. Personal Services	22.5	13.4	13.8	8.8	10.3	8.8	15.5	9.9
6. Professional Services	4.3	1.5	13.3	12.3	31.5	32.1	14.9	14.7
7. Banking/ Insurance	2.2	1.1	7.8	9.2	9.6	9.4	6.6	7.4
8. Others	4.2	13.0	8.6	15.1	10.2	13.4	8.2	14.2
Total %	*100*	*100*	*100*	*100*	*100*	*100*	*100*	*100*
N	*438*	*301*	*744*	*662*	*346*	*317*	*1528*	*1280*

For those with pre-Leaving Certificate qualifications, most of the decline is accounted for either by movement to unemployment or out of the labour force altogether, with the actual number employed in retail/wholesale and personal services, for instance, declining by over half from first to current job. Even for "growing" industries, like manufacturing and construction, there is actually a decline in the numbers employed between first job and current job of around 15 per cent. Most of the poorly qualified who left jobs in the secondary sectors of the labour market (mostly personal services and retail/ wholesale), therefore, have become unemployed or actually retired from the labour force altogether. Most of the former are men; most of the latter, women.

For those with a Leaving Certificate qualification, the decline in "secondary sector" industrial employment is not as dramatic, with unemployment or withdrawal from the labour force not nearly as serious; while there is significant growth in numbers in manufacturing and other higher-paying industries. For third level graduates, the situation is even more satisfactory, with a significant decline in secondary sector jobs and significant growth in professional service, banking/insurance and manufacturing employment from first to current job. (Appendix Tables A6.1 to A6.3 contain more detailed breakdowns by educational level.)

MEASURING LABOUR MARKET SEGMENTATION

We use Hughes and Nolan's (1997) adaptation of the more refined Gordon (1986), and Gordon, Edwards and Reich (1982) conceptual and measurement approach to their four-segment model of the United States economy. This uses both industrial and occupational data available from US census sources to classify jobs into sectors, starting with a fourfold (2×2) classification of occupations (semi-skilled/unskilled and others) and industries (core and peripheral), classified according to the characteristics of their products or product markets (goods-producing/others, etc.):

1. *Independent primary professional/technical:* higher technical/professional occupations in core industries in which workers control their activities, have high education/training requirements, and have high degrees of autonomy.

2. *Independent primary craft:* intermediate technical and skilled/craft jobs in core industries. These have a high degree of independence/autonomy, have frequent changes of activity (less routinised), and high occupational specific training (greater than two years) requirements.

3. *Subordinate primary:* less control and non-routinised jobs in primary segment, and unskilled/semi-skilled manual/service occupations in goods-producing sectors.

4. *Secondary sector:* peripheral industries, and unskilled/semi-skilled manual/service occupations in non-goods-producing industries. Besides industrial sector, the other main distinction between categories 3 and 4 is the extent of training time required — more or less than three months (Gordon, 1986).

In this classification, industry alone determines segment location for unskilled and semi-skilled "blue collar" occupations. In all other (industry by occupation) categories, occupational characteristics mainly determine segment location (Gordon, 1986). Occupations are scored on the bases of their degree of autonomy, extent of repetitiveness/routinisation in their job tasks, extent of vocational training/preparation required to carry out work roles, etc.

Surprisingly, the distribution of employment in the four sectors for Ireland and the US are very similar (Hughes and Nolan, 1997). Using the same occupational/industrial coding, the distribution of school leavers in their first, first permanent and current jobs are given below, showing the comparison with the adult labour force as categorised by Hughes and Nolan (1997).

Table 6.3: Distribution of Employment in Four Labour Market Segments for First Job, First Permanent Job, Current Job, by Sex (comparison with adult distribution)

Labour Market Segment	**First Job**		**First Permanent Job**		**Current Job**		**Adults***
	Male	*Female*	*Male*	*Female*	*Male*	*Female*	
	%	%	%	%	%	%	%
1. Independent Primary Professional/ Technical	18.8	14.1	20.7	18.0	26.9	25.9	25.4
2. Independent Primary Craft	14.5	1.6	16.9	2.1	16.3	3.3	16.9
3. Subordinate Primary	17.0	26.4	18.7	28.9	24.7	29.3	35.0
4. Secondary	49.7	57.9	43.7	51.0	32.1	41.0	25.7
Total %	*100*	*100*	*100*	*100*	*100*	*100*	
N	*811*	*768*	*782*	*740*	*648*	*625*	

* Hughes and Nolan, 1997, p. 13.

Some very clear distinctions between the youth and adult distributions, between the female and male distribution, and changes over time in the youth distributions, are apparent:

- A much higher percentage of youth are in the secondary sector: over 50 per cent for first job. This contrasts with less than 26 per cent for adults. So in their first period in the labour market, young people are more than twice as likely to find jobs in the secondary sector of the economy.
- This concentration declines substantially over time from first job to current job: from 50 to 32 per cent for males, and from 58 to 41 per cent for females, the decline being somewhat more pronounced for males.
- Females are much more likely to be concentrated in the secondary sector — primarily in clerical jobs and in low-skilled service employment (corresponding to the Hughes and Nolan, 1997, study). They are almost absent from the independent primary craft sector. So, despite their higher level of education, they are disproportionately concentrated in the secondary sector.
- There is an apparent significant upward shift over time from the secondary sector to the subordinate primary sector, particularly for males; and a significant growth over time in the primary professional/technical sector.
- However, a significant proportion of those initially employed — particularly in the secondary sector — become unemployed over time or, amongst females, withdraw completely from the labour force. We examine this issue in detail in a later section. However, we first examine the aggregate changes by level of education.

Changes in Segment by Educational Level

Analysing such segment changes by educational level shows three very clear patterns (Table 6.4).

Being in the secondary segment is highly correlated with level of education, as we have already seen. Almost 60 per cent of those with a Leaving Certificate or less start off in the secondary segment in their first jobs, declining to over 40 per cent for current job — six years after entering the labour market for the first time.

The main sector increases for those with a Leaving Certificate occur in the "subordinate primary" and "professional/technical" categories, increasing from 32 to 40 per cent. As already indicated, most of the changes in distribution for those with less than a Leaving

Certificate, and particularly for those with no qualifications, are into unemployment or withdrawal from the labour force.

Table 6.4: Distribution of Employment in Four Labour Market Segments for First Job, First Permanent Job, Current Job, by Level of Education

Labour Market Segment	**First Job**			**First Permanent Job**			**Current Job**			**Adults***
	Pre LC %	*LC* %	*Third Level* %	*Pre LC* %	*LC* %	*Third Level* %	*Pre LC* %	*LC* %	*Third Level* %	%
1. Independent Primary Professional/ Technical	5.1	10.2	43.6	5.3	11.4	54.3	8.4	18.7	59.6	25.4
2. Independent Primary Craft	13.2	7.4	3.7	15.0	9.0	4.5	16.1	10.1	3.7	16.9
3. Subordinate Primary	24.0	22.1	17.5	25.3	26.1	16.2	30.5	30.2	17.7	35.0
4. Secondary	57.1	60.3	35.2	54.3	53.5	25.0	44.9	41.1	19.0	25.7
Total %	*100*	*100*	*100*	*100*	*100*	*100*	*100*	*100*	*100*	
N	*457*	*752*	*370*	*438*	*740*	*345*	*299*	*658*	*315*	

* Hughes and Nolan, 1997, p. 13.

Professional/technical occupations are the prerogative of third level (particularly university) graduates (see also Appendix Table A6.1 to A6.3), the percentage in this segment increasing from 44 to 60 per cent from first to current job, with an almost proportionate decline in the secondary segment. So, as in previous analyses, it appears that a significant minority of third level graduates (over one-third) take up jobs in the secondary segment, but gradually move out of them as time in the labour force increases. Nevertheless, even for current jobs, almost one-fifth are in the secondary sector. Many of these, however, have spent little time in the labour force, and some others are in middle-level positions in secondary industries.

These results come only from simple one- and two-way cross-classifications; however, they do suggest considerable educational differences in segment location and an upward mobility out of the secondary segment over time. For those in "current jobs", six years after entering the labour market, those with a Leaving Certificate or less are still almost twice as likely (at 41 per cent) to be in the secondary segment of the labour force than the adult workforce as a whole (at 26 per cent). Whether such initial entry to the secondary segment of the labour market has such important constraining effects on upward career mobility, as the research literature suggests, will be explored in detail in a subsequent section. However, before we examine in detail the effects of initial sector location on subsequent employment chances, career mobility or labour force withdrawal, we need to test whether these industry/occupational sector distinctions have any predictive validity in terms of one of the main hypotheses of the model: that earnings are determined differently in the primary and secondary segments.

Segmentation Theory and Earnings

In the conventional, human capital, individualistic model, earnings are hypothesised to be mainly a function of an individual's education/training and work experience, irrespective of industry or sector. One of the main hypotheses of segmentation theory, on the other hand, is that earnings of workers are determined differently in primary than in secondary segments. According to this hypothesis, the primary sector not only pays higher wages, it also yields high rates of return to education, while the secondary sector, with lower wage rates, yields a much lower rate of return to education and work experience (Doeringer and Piore, 1971; Gordon *et al.*, 1982; Waitzman and Smith, 1994; Hughes and Nolan, 1997). In Table 6.5, we use a three-segment comparison — amalgamating subordinate primary with primary craft because of small numbers — to test for the differential effects of education and work experience on earnings.

The results do indeed show, as does the Hughes and Nolan (1997) research, that educational returns are much lower in the secondary and subordinate primary and primary-craft sectors than in the primary-professional/technical sector. The coefficient for the latter is between two and three times greater than for the former sector. The F tests for the hypothesis — that the three sub-sample regression coefficients come from the same population — show a clear rejection of the hypothesis. Interestingly, gender and percentage of time in the labour market employed also show significant sector differences.

Table 6.5: Regression of Earnings (Log of Gross Earnings Per Hour) on a Set of Explanatory Variables (for the full sample and three labour market segments)

Variables		**Labour Market Segment**		
	Full Sample	*Independent Primary, Professional/ Technical*	*Independent Primary, Craft and Subordinate Primary Sector*	*Secondary Sector*
1. Constant	.68**	.73**	.95**	.84**
2. Gender (1=Female, 0=Male)	–.05	.08	–.14**	–.01
3. Level of Education	.06**	.10**	.04**	.03*
4. Percentage of Time Employed†	.25**	–.22	.37**	.11
5. Full or Part-Time Employed	.03	.05	–.09	.01
6. Size of Firm	.08**	.08**	.07**	.09**
Adjusted R^2	.25	.23	.28	.18
N	738	172	302	261

† Percentage of time in labour force employed is used instead of time employed/unemployed, as the latter measures have either too little variance (because within educational levels school leavers entered the labour market at the same time) or because the variance present is so highly correlated with level of education, that it has no consistent effect. The nature of our sample does not, therefore, allow for testing of time employed/unemployed effects.
* p <.05; ** p<.01

Females have significantly lower earnings in the independent-primary-craft subordinate-primary sectors — mainly, it appears, because of the greater significance of skilled manual employment for males and of lower medium-term earning returns for females in clerical employment. Percentage of time employed is also strongly associated with higher earnings in the subordinate-primary/ primary-craft sectors, but not in others. While this result is supportive of the hypothesis of *lower earnings returns* to work experience in the secondary sector, the results for the primary professional/ technical sector do not support the hypothesis. There is, of course, much lower variance in this variable in the latter sector — primarily because of the much higher proportion of third level graduates in it, their high employment rate and their shorter time in the labour market. With these exceptions, however, the results strongly support the central hypothesis of the segmentation model: that there are significant sector differences in the way earnings are determined, particularly in the importance of education; and that such sectoral distinctions are very significant in the Irish youth labour market.

Effects of Initial Sectoral Location on Movement into Unemployment and Other Statuses

A significant minority of people, as we have seen, had become unemployed or had withdrawn from the labour force into "other statuses" (mostly into "home duties") by the time of the 1992 re-survey. In the following regression (Table 6.6), we estimate the relationship between initial social background factors, educational level achieved, initial location in the secondary sector of the economy for first (permanent) job, and current (1992) economic status (divided according to whether (i) unemployed, or (ii) in "other statuses"). The hypothesis proposed is that, controlling for other relevant factors, those initially employed in the secondary sector are more likely to become unemployed or move into other statuses. The latter is expected to be almost exclusively characteristic of females. We use logistic regression to estimate the effects, testing particularly for the effects of original (first permanent job) location in the "secondary sector" or in the "subordinate primary sector".

The results are very clear and contrary to our hypotheses in both cases. Withdrawal from the labour force is not correlated with secondary sector location for first (permanent) jobs once the effects of level of education and other relevant variables have been controlled for. It is highly associated with educational level, gender and father's unemployment. Young women, the more poorly educated and those whose fathers were unemployed, are far more likely to have withdrawn from the labour force. It is not so much sector that is important, therefore, but educational level and other job history characteristics, as well as other socio-economic and socio-cultural background factors, as they particularly affect young women in the initial post-school phase of the lifecycle (see Hannan and Ó Riain, 1993).

Table 6.6: Results of Logistic Regression Predicting: (i) Withdrawal from the Labour Force, and (ii) Current Unemployment from a Set of Social Background, Educational Achievement and Location in the Secondary Segment of the Labour Market for First Permanent Job

Independent Variables	**Currently in "Other Statuses" (=1, Else=0)**	**Employment Status (Unemployed=1, Employed=0)**
1. Father's Occupational Status	.01	–.02
2. Father's Unemployment (Unemployed=1; Else=0)	.84**	.39**
3. Gender (Female=1, Male=0)	3.45**	–.57
4. Level of Education Achieved	–.39**	–.24**
5. Initial (First Permanent Job) Location in Secondary Sector	–.09	.17
6. Constant	–8.40**	.60
– 2 Log Likelihood	*382.8*	*1037.3*
Improvement	*109.3***	*106.7***
N	*1466*	*1384*

* p <.05; ** p<.01

Secondary sector location for first jobs has no effect either on current employment chances, restricting consideration to those currently in the labour force. Much the same set of variables have the expected effects, particularly educational level and fathers being unemployed. Gender, however, has no independent effect. Therefore, being female disproportionately affects withdrawal, but young women remaining in the labour force continue to have the same employment chances as males.

In the next section, we test a related hypothesis: that initial entry to the secondary sector negatively affects the probability of upward career mobility from first to current job.

The Effects of Initial Entry to Labour Market Segment on Subsequent Career Mobility

As in Chapter 4, we use multiple regression methods to test for the effects of initial labour market segment entered on subsequent occupational achievement. The results there showed that, controlling for educational level achieved and all relevant social background variables, the occupational status of first job entered has the most important effect of all variables on current occupational status achieved. So, third level graduates who initially took up lower status jobs have significantly lower current occupational status levels than those entering at a higher level, irrespective of the effects of all other control variables. The hypothesis tested here is that initial entry to the secondary (or the "subordinate primary") sector has significant additional constraining effects on upward career mobility. In Table 6.7, we first examine the additional effects of labour market segment initially entered — controlling for all other relevant variables, including occupational status of first job — on current occupational status achieved. The control variables included are those found to be significant in Table 5.1.

Equation 1 shows that four variables combined explain 54 per cent of the variance in current occupational status levels: occupational status of first job (by far the most important); educational level achieved; mother's educational level; and gender. Initial educational level and initial occupational status have both joint and independent effects. Controlling for educational level and other relevant variables, the lower the status or quality of initial jobs, the lower the current occupational status. Even controlling for the latter, the higher the educational level, the greater the status of current job. So, point of initial entry to the labour market has persistent effects, while educational level continues to have additional and continuing effects well beyond entry status. In addition, however, mother's educational status has an additional positive effect — whether a cultural or a resource effect, it is not possible to say from our data. Finally, being a woman has a significant negative effect on current occupational status. Even with the same education and the same initial occupational status achieved, women have lower rates of upward mobility than men, though having a slight advantage on first entry to the labour market (see also Table 5.1).

Table 6.7: Regression of Current Occupational Status on SES of Origin, Mother's Education, Educational Level, Gender, Occupational Status and Labour Market Segment Entered

	Equation 1	**Equation 2**	**Equation 3**
Independent Variables	*Occupational Status of Current Job*		
A. Socio-economic & Socio-cultural Background Variables	β	β	β
1. Mother's Educational Level	.81*	1.03**	.79*
2. Respondent's Gender (1=Female; 0=Male)	–1.14**	1.14	–1.23**
B. Level of Educational Achievement of Respondent			
3. Level of Educational Achievement	2.6**	3.88**	2.44**
C. Occupational Status Achieved			
4. Occupational Status of First Permanent Job	.56**	–	.54**
D. Labour Market Segmentation (First Permanent Job)†			
5. Independent Primary Craft	–	–9.25**	–3.16*
6. Subordinate Primary	–	–11.32**	–1.86
7. Secondary	–	–14.31**	–1.27
R^2 =	*0.54*	*0.45*	*0.54*
df =	*4/1163*	*6/1161*	*7/1160*
p =	*<.001*	*<.001*	*<.001*

† Reference Category = Professional/Technical Sector; * p < .05; ** p < 0.1.

In equation 2, we test for the main effect of initial labour market segment location, excluding occupational status of first job from the equation. The results show very strong negative effects of secondary, subordinate primary and even primary craft locations on current occupational statuses, controlling for level of education and SES of origin, etc. So in this respect at least, the hypothesis is strongly supported. However, the percentage of overall variance explained is substantially lower than in equation 1. The cruder categorical nature of the segmentation variable captures less of the variance in initial relevant occupational experience than does the overall occupational status scale.

In equation 3, we use both sets of initial labour market status variables: occupational status of first job and initial labour market segment entered. The addition of the labour market segment variables has minimal effect on the regression coefficients for the preceding variables, and adds very little to the explained variance in equation 1 (although having a first job in the primary craft segment does have a small additional negative effect on occupational mobility). The effect, however, is barely statistically significant. If labour market segment has an independent negative effect, it appears to be almost completely captured by the occupational status variable used. This does use both occupation and industry in its construction (Hope and Goldthorpe, 1974). In Appendix Table A6.4, we show the intercorrelations amongst these two independent variables. Being in a secondary segment, for instance, has a highly negative correlation (r = –.56) with occupational status of first job; the distribution of occupations in that segment is almost fully confined to lower skilled manual/service occupations. So the effects of segment location are almost fully mediated by the occupational status scale. Therefore, although our main hypothesis is strongly supported by the results in equation 2, it is clear from the results of equation 3 that the continuous occupational status scale not only captures almost all of the effects of sectoral location, but also explains far more of the variance in current occupational status. So, in statistical terms at least, the occupational status scale is a more "explanatory" measure.

Of course, the Hope-Goldthorpe occupational status scale incorporates popular judgements of the socio-economic (dis)advantages associated with individual occupational-industrial categories, and incorporates many of the same underlying dimensions in its construction, as does the Gordon (1986) four-segment model. There is, therefore, a not unexpected, pronounced association between individual occupational/industrial allocations in the Gordon segmentation model and the Hope-Goldthorpe occupational status scale. Appendix Table A6.4 contains the details. It shows that most secondary sector jobs are semi-skilled and unskilled manual and service jobs — with a median occupational status equivalent to semi-skilled manual or personal service occupations, the value of the upper interquartile range being less than that of most clerical occupations. At the other extreme, the predominance of higher technical/professional occupations in the "Independent Primary:

professional/technical" category is equally marked. Given this high association and the much greater discrimination of the occupational status scale, it, not unexpectedly, captures almost all the effects of the sectoral location variable.

The most reasonable interpretation of the results of Table 6.7, therefore, is that initial location in lower status, "secondary segment" jobs does have a clear negative effect on subsequent upward mobility chances, but that the boundary or threshold between this occupational/industrial segment and others is not experienced as sharply as the segmentation literature suggests. Variation in the quality of the job/occupation first taken, irrespective of industrial/ firm location, appears to be more predictive of upward career mobility than sector location *per se*. In statistical terms, therefore, there appears to be no clear-cut boundary between "good job" and "bad job" sectors that adds independently to the explanatory power of the continuous occupational status scale.

In conceptual or theoretical terms, however, segmentation theory does put flesh on the underlying economic explanation for the "lower status" and lower wages/conditions of those workers at the bottom of the pile, with very poor jobs in non-goods-producing and highly competitive service sectors dominated by small firms. It also provides explanations for the better wages/conditions and higher occupational statuses of those at the top of the pile — in primary sector professional/technical occupations (see Gordon *et al.*, 1982). In focusing attention on structural features of the labour market, it provides additional explanations as to why it appears to be difficult to escape from lower status and low wage and occupational/ industrial sectors.

Overqualification and Sector

What is the relevance of sectoral analysis to the "overqualification" issue? The main one is that around two-thirds of third level graduates who take jobs for which they are "overqualified" are in secondary sector jobs: 86 per cent of those with degrees and 54 per cent of those with certificates/diplomas (see Appendix Table A6.5). These low-status jobs in insecure sectors of the economy, predominantly occupied by those with second level qualifications, are usually taken up only as a last resort by third level graduates. Overqualification, therefore, for third level graduates and even for those with a Leaving Certificate mainly means taking jobs in the secondary sector. What this chapter describes and explains, therefore, is the particularly disadvantaged labour market demand characteristics of those sectors in which most of the "overqualified" work; as well of course as the more permanently disadvantaged position of the more poorly educated.

SUMMARY

On first entry to the labour market, around 40 per cent of all school/college leavers take up lower status occupations in the retail/wholesale and personal service industries or, using more precise industry-by-occupation classifications, over half enter the weaker "secondary sectors" of the labour market — almost twice the proportion as in the adult labour force (see Tables 6.1, 6.3). So there is a high degree of youth/adult segmentation in the Irish labour market, with a significant proportion of such "youth jobs" in the secondary sector appearing to be temporary — being constantly re-circulated amongst first entrants in the labour market.

This tendency, or necessity, to take up such poorly rewarded, low-prospect, secondary-sector jobs in the first period in the labour market is highly correlated with level of education. The rate for those with no qualifications is almost double that of those with third level qualifications. Nevertheless, over a third of third level graduates take up their first jobs in the secondary sector, the great majority of whom are in positions for which they are clearly overqualified. In an overcrowded labour market, where employers appear to pay inordinate attention to level of education achieved in making employment decisions, those with good Leaving Certificate, and even third level qualifications, compete with the more poorly educated for unskilled and semi-skilled manual and service jobs, at least for the "first jobs" period in the labour market.

Although this concentration in lower-status, secondary-sector jobs declines substantially over time for third level graduates — by almost half over a two- to three-year period — almost one-in-five third level graduates are still in secondary sector jobs a number of years later. The decline — from first job — is almost by 50 per cent for those with third level qualifications, and by almost a third for those with a Leaving Certificate. For those with lower level qualifications, the decline is substantially lower. So, not only are the more poorly qualified much more likely to enter "secondary sector" jobs, they even have to compete with much more highly educated young adults to get these jobs, and they are far more likely to remain captured in that lower-paying and lower-prospect sector than are their more educationally fortunate peers. In addition, however, since these jobs are much less secure — more temporary, more part-time and more subject to unemployment — they are far more likely to subsequently become unemployed and to retire from the labour force altogether (see Table 6.6, and Hannan and Ó Riain, 1993). What appears to be occurring is that a significant proportion of such low-skilled jobs in the wholesale/retail and personal services sectors are given only on a temporary basis, and are being "recirculated" to succeeding cohorts of young school/college leavers. Employers appear to be attempting to maximise their chances of getting more highly educated youth on a temporary basis rather than offering permanent jobs to less-educated — though adequately qualified — youth. Because of an over-supply of those with Leaving Certificate and higher qualifications, up to the early 1990s, those with low-level or no qualifications were effectively being excluded from the labour market.

Two underlying "human capital" rationales for such employer behaviour suggest themselves:

(i) Employers try to maximise the "general human capital" level of their employment intake — in literacy and numeracy levels, but also the higher social/cultural capital aspects of more highly educated youth.

(ii) They attempt to minimise their own training costs, as well as their provision of more permanent jobs with career prospects.

This secondary sector employers' strategy appears rational and understandable in times of substantial over-supply of highly educated youth labour. It makes little sense in the medium to long term, however, as labour supply starts to decline and employment expands from the late 1990s onwards. In addition, such rapid turnover of highly educated but poorly trained labour cannot have many long-term employer benefits, except in very insecure sectors with short firm lives.

From the point of view of the better-educated employee, such initial entry to the secondary sector of the labour market has few advantages. Leaving Certificate and third level graduates who initially take up such lower status, or secondary sector jobs, are substantially less likely to achieve higher status occupational levels than those who first entered at a higher and more "level congruent" position.

To conclude, therefore, the segmentation approach, in focusing on characteristics of the demand side of the youth labour market, puts significant explanatory meat on the differentiated processes underlying labour market entry trajectories — even if it does not statistically add to the amount of variance explained by the older, individualistic, "occupational attainment" model.

Chapter 7

Summary and Conclusions

INTRODUCTION

This chapter summarises the results of our analyses of a follow-up survey of school/college leavers, who completed their second level education in 1985/86 and were last interviewed in late 1992. The main policy question guiding the research is the extent to which Irish third level graduates take up jobs more characteristic of those with lower level qualifications. Given the high degree of "qualification inflation" that has occurred in the Irish labour market since the early 1980s (Breen, 1984a; Hannan, 1986; Canny *et al.*, 1995), and the extent to which qualifications and grades are used for appointments even to lower level jobs (Breen *et al.*, 1995) one would expect a significant degree of "overqualification" amongst those taking up low-skilled occupations for their first jobs. If this is substantially present, however, it would indicate not only low rates of return to their education for the individuals concerned, but also low overall social rates of return to the state's increased expenditure on third level education since the early 1980s.

Three broad research questions and their associated hypotheses guided the research:

(i) What is the degree of "level congruence" between the level of education attained and the occupational status achieved on entry to the labour market?

In guiding the analyses to answer this research question, three linked hypotheses were proposed:

a) There is a high degree of "level congruence" between level of education and occupational status of jobs achieved, with high rates of return to increasing levels of education in both employment chances and in occupational status achieved.

b) However, there would, nevertheless, be a moderate to high degree of "overqualification" amongst third level entrants to the labour market, particularly in the "first job" phase.

c) This would, however, decline rapidly with time in the labour market.

While third level qualifications are either essential to, or highly desirable for, access to the upper sectors of the Irish labour market, such upper status positions are significantly rationed, often require considerable work experience, and are difficult to achieve on first entry to the labour market. Because of this, the substantial overcrowding in the Irish youth labour market and the greater extent to which Irish employers use educational credentials in their employment decisions (Breen *et al.*, 1995), a significant minority of third level graduates are expected to take up their first jobs in lower status occupations for which the main recruitment is from those with second level qualifications. However, if such "overqualification" exists in the Irish youth labour market, does it persist or is it only characteristic of the "first jobs" phase following labour market entry, as some international evidence suggests?

(ii) Secondly, if such a phenomenon exists in the Irish youth labour market, what are the main effects of such initial "overqualification" for individuals' subsequent careers; and what are the implications for educational and labour market policy?

Two relevant hypotheses are proposed:

d) Those who take up occupations for which they are "overqualified" will have lower career mobility chances than those entering educationally congruent occupations.

e) However, the more highly educated who remain in lower status jobs are expected to get higher wages/salaries than their more poorly educated peers because of their greater human capital.

(iii) These hypotheses, however, refer only to the characteristics of job seekers. On the demand side of the labour market, the main distinctions expected to be important are differences in individuals' industrial/occupational locations or labour market segments. Most recent international

studies show significant youth/adult differences in labour market positions, with youth disproportionately concentrated in the secondary industrial/occupational segments.

It was hypothesised, therefore, that:

f) Those who are "overqualified" for their first jobs would be concentrated in the secondary sector of the labour market, in which returns to education are substantially lower. Location, in this sector, significantly depresses subsequent upward career mobility. Such secondary industrial/occupational segments are expected, therefore, to have relatively impermeable boundaries, and location within them is expected to offer lower earnings returns (see Chapter 6 for review).

Methods, Data

The analyses are based on a national survey of school leavers from 1985/86 who were first interviewed in May 1987 (N = 2,089) and secondly in late 1992 (N = 1,659) — one and six years respectively after they had completed their second level education. Except for 15 per cent of third level respondents still in college at the time of the interview, around 98 per cent of the cohort had at some time entered the labour market; though almost a third of very poorly educated young women had withdrawn from it by the time of the 1992 interview.

Quality of jobs is measured by their "occupational status" in terms of a scale which scores occupations in terms of the skill levels and degree of autonomy and control exercised by workers within the occupation, the earnings yielded, the average level of education of workers within them, and the associated perceived level of prestige that the average person holding the occupation enjoys. The occupational status scale we use is the 36-value Hope-Goldthorpe (1974) occupational status scale. This yields a hierarchically stratified order of occupational categories which varies in (equally appearing) interval level scores from unskilled manual/service occupations (value = 18) to a top value of 72 for higher professional occupations (see Table 2.5).

Being "overqualified" for a job is defined as occurring when a person with a higher level of qualification takes up an occupation at a level more characteristic of those with a lower level qualification: for instance, those with a third level certificate qualification whose occupations are at or below the median value of those with a Leaving Certificate qualification. In other words, we define it as occurring when those with higher level qualifications have jobs/occupations they could apparently have achieved with lower level qualifications. Using this definition, around 40 per cent of respondents in their first jobs are clearly "overqualified" for them, declining to around 20 per cent of those in current (1992) jobs. So it is quite a significant phenomenon, though declining rapidly with time in the labour market.

MAIN RESULTS

We present the summary of the results and conclusions in four sections: (i) post-school educational/training attainments; (ii) initial labour market histories of the cohort; (iii) factors affecting initial educational and occupational career mobility, including the effects of initial "overqualification" on career mobility; and (iv) market and structural factors affecting careers and earnings, particularly the effects of initial secondary sector location.

(i) Post-School Educational/Training Attainments

The results demonstrate what an extremely time-bound and rigidly stratified educational system we have in Ireland. Only around five per cent of those who left school before the Leaving Certificate, for instance, ever returned to get higher level qualifications in the six years following their leaving school. The higher the level of initial education completed, the greater the chances of subsequently improving that level. Post-school vocational training was somewhat more re-distributive, but only around ten per cent of the cohort got any such qualifications. Compared to many other OECD countries, we have an extremely low level of post-school part-time or full-time education for those not going on to third level education (Nakajima, 1990; Hannan *et al.*, 1996).

Entry to the labour market was almost immediate for all school leavers not going on to third level education or other full-time education/training courses. The median, and modal, year of first job was 1986 for second level school leavers, 1988 for those graduating with a third level certificate qualification, 1989 for those with diplomas and 1990 for those with degrees. Almost 90 per cent of third level graduates took up their studies immediately on completing their second level education. Even for those with Leaving Certificate qualifications, educational "second chances" are very rare if not taken up immediately on leaving school and they are almost completely absent for those with lower level qualifications.

(ii) Early Labour Market Experience

The main differentiating labour market experience amongst school leavers with varying levels of education is whether they got any job at all: with almost one-in-four "early leavers", without any qualification, never getting any job — an outcome almost absent for everybody else. In addition, the time to first job, the rate of subsequent loss of employment and overall time spent unemployed are almost equally discriminatory. Even excluding those who never got any job, average time to first job is 50 per cent longer for those without qualifications than for those with a Leaving Certificate. Leaving Certificate graduates with the same (six years) labour market experience as the less qualified were more than ten times less likely to have never got a job, and more than six times less likely to be unemployed or to have withdrawn from the labour force six years out from school. Taking time in the labour force into account, third level graduates are even more advantaged.

Job search is quite dispersed geographically. A high proportion — almost a third — of the total cohort emigrated at some time during the six years since leaving second level education; though only 15 per cent were still abroad at the time of interview in 1992. Internal migration is also very high, particularly at the initial job search stage. Such migration does not, however, appear to be motivated by alienation from one's home community, but by failure to find an acceptable occupation and earnings living there (see also Sexton *et al.*, 1991). Indeed, as we shall see later, the evidence generally suggests that, given a reasonable job offer, most young people are willing to pay a price to stay on in their local community.

(iii) Education/Occupation "Matching" and "Overqualification"

The extent to which respondents from different educational levels enter the same labour market, competing with each other in an open, competitive market, is one of the main questions of this research. In fact, Irish labour market entry is quite stratified, with the more highly educated on average entering higher level occupational niches than the more poorly educated (see also Breen, 1984a; Breen *et al.*, 1995; Smyth and Surridge, 1996). The majority of university graduates do not compete in the same labour market as those with a Leaving Certificate, and on average the latter do not compete for the low-skilled manual/service occupations characteristic of those with junior cycle or lower qualifications (see Appendix Tables A4.1 to A4.3). There is a moderate to high correlation between level of education and occupational status achieved; this correlation increases with time in the labour force. There is, nevertheless, significant overlap between educational levels in occupations entered, particularly for first jobs.

As already indicated, there is considerable variance in the range of occupations entered by all educational levels, with significant occupational "overlap", for instance, between those with junior cycle and Leaving Certificate qualifications, and between the latter and those with third level qualifications (see Appendix Tables A4.2 to A4.4). The extent of occupational overlap or similarity between different educational levels decreases with level of education. It is most characteristic of those with a Leaving Certificate and least characteristic of those with a university degree. This occupational "overlap" also decreases more rapidly over time for the more highly educated. The average employer, therefore, does discriminate quite strongly between educational levels in initial employment decisions and appears quite willing to appoint more highly qualified applicants to posts where the average educational requirements are much lower. So, only the better educated get the better jobs but, given the substantial over-supply of first job applicants with higher qualifications in the late 1980s and early 1990s (a situation no longer holding), employers appear equally willing to choose the most qualified for even the least skilled jobs. However, although third level graduates taking up low status jobs do pay some price for so doing in terms of subsequent mobility chances, taking up initial jobs for which they were clearly overqualified does not create additional barriers.

With increasing time in the labour market, substantial upward career mobility occurs; the higher the level of education, the greater the degree of such upward movement. For example, two-thirds of those with third level qualifications who initially took up manual or lower status service occupations were subsequently upwardly mobile into non-manual jobs, with little upward mobility occurring amongst the least qualified. Career stability and downward mobility, as well as unemployment and even movement out of the labour force altogether, is more characteristic of those with less than a Leaving Certificate. For example, almost two out of three of those with no qualifications were either unemployed or had actually withdrawn from the labour force by 1992, compared to less than ten per cent of those with third level qualifications (Table 4.3).

As a result of these changes in status over the first few years in the labour market, the extent to which those with higher level qualifications take jobs for which they are "overqualified" declines sharply from first job (47 per cent) to current job (26 per cent) for those with Leaving Certificate qualifications, and from 43 to 21 per cent for those with degrees. The correlations, therefore, between educational level and occupational status achieved increases over time in the labour market — at least for the first three to five years in it. Although there has been a substantial degree of "qualification inflation" over the last 15 to 20 years (Breen, 1984a; Hannan, 1986; Sexton *et al.*, 1996; Duggan *et al.*, 1997), the relative labour market advantages of higher versus lower qualifications continues to hold, particularly with increasing time in the labour market.

Even after a number of years at work, however, a significant minority of third level graduates are still in jobs for which they are clearly overqualified. It may be of course that this residual group is negatively selected — in that they have unmeasured personal characteristics and work experiences which militate against internal promotions or external appointments. Educational level clearly does not measure all relevant employment/promotion personal characteristics. Staying on in jobs for which one is overqualified, of course, could also be a matter of choice, or unavoidable constraint on choice. Some respondents either may not want to or, for family and other reasons, are unable to move to other places, even within Ireland, where "more suitable" and more highly rewarded jobs are available.

(iv) The Relative Effects of Educational Level and Other Factors on Occupational Achievement

In Chapter 5, we presented the results of detailed multivariate analyses of the factors affecting educational achievement, first and current occupational status as well as current earnings levels. In addition, the effects of initial "overeducation" — in first jobs — on subsequent career chances were examined in detail. We briefly summarise the main results below:

- Educational achievement is significantly structured by the socio-economic and socio-cultural resources of families (see also Hannan *et al.*, 1996).
- Occupational status of first job is substantially influenced by educational level achieved, but also to a lesser extent by the socio-cultural resources of the family of origin.
- Current occupational status is mainly determined by the status of first job achieved, controlling for educational level, although educational level achieved does retain continuing influence: the minority of the more highly educated who initially take up lower status jobs do pay a price in terms of subsequent upward mobility chances.
- Once educational level and occupational status of first job are controlled for, being "overeducated" for first job has no additional negative effect on subsequent occupational achievement, as had been hypothesised. It is the effect of having lower status jobs that is important, not any additional penalty paid, where these jobs are more typical of those with lower level qualifications.
- Labour market location has a significant effect on occupational achievement and earnings. Those who stay on locally in non-Dublin locations pay a significant price in lower occupational statuses and incomes for so doing. The national labour market, with Dublin at its apex, both recruits on a national scale — using more formal methods — and yields higher returns on educational investments.

These and earlier results (Sexton *et al.*, 1991) do indicate, however, a high degree of willingness amongst Irish school leavers to trade initial occupational advancement against local/regional employment — within, however, a reasonable range of occupations and wage rates. For most school/college leavers also, emigration appears to be either a conscious short-range choice or a decision arrived at only after failure to get a job at home; and most appear willing to return home as soon as opportunities become available, or after they have also failed to get employment abroad (see Hannan and Ó Riain, 1993).

- "Surplus" human capital — as indicated by being "over-qualified" for one's job — does not yield any additional earnings to the individual. The hypothesis of such an additional return to surplus human capital is, therefore, clearly rejected. Indeed, for those individuals who remain on in such jobs, there are significant negative earnings effects. It may well be, of course, that these respondents who remain on in jobs for which they are overqualified have many other unmeasured personal qualities which would explain both their lower levels of occupational achievement and lower earnings.
- There is no evidence that vocational/technical subject specialisations at second level yield additional labour market returns, though there is a clear advantage to professional/technical qualifications at third level. The general lack of correspondence or "content congruence" between what one does at (second level) school and what job one gets subsequently is a particular disadvantage to young people of working class origins with poor educational levels and grades. This contrasts sharply with the experience of many continental European countries (Müller *et al.*, 1996; Shavit and Müller, 1998).

(v) Overqualification and Labour Market Segment

In Chapter 6, we reported the results of our analyses of the nature and effects of labour market segment entered — particularly the effects of entry to the "secondary sector" of the labour market (mostly semi-skilled or unskilled jobs in retail/wholesale, restaurant, hotel and other personal service industries). The percentage of youth (under-25s) in these sectors is more than twice that of adults, with a lot of the jobs being temporary and constantly re-circulated.

- Most "overqualified" respondents are in such secondary segment jobs; and it is in this segment also that most of the competition between young people with different levels of education occurs.
- Labour market segment entered has significantly different effects on earnings returns to education, with earnings returns being much lower in the secondary than in the primary professional/ technical segment.
- Segment entered is highly correlated with educational level, with secondary segment location being least characteristic of those educated at third level. Location in the secondary segment also declines rapidly with increasing time in the labour market, with mobility out of it highly dependent on educational level achieved.
- The hypothesis that initially entering a "secondary" labour market segment has significant constraining effects on upward career mobility is strongly supported by our data. However, the correlation between low occupational status and secondary sector location is high, so once occupational status is controlled for in any of the regression equations, secondary sector location has no additional effect on upward career mobility chances or earnings growth. The hypothesis of a specific sectoral constraint on upward mobility, independent of occupational status, is not supported.
- Despite this statistical weakness, however, the use of the labour market segmentation model is very revealing. In focusing on the structural characteristics of the youth labour market, it reveals the underlying economic and employer behaviour determinants of youth employment in those sectors where it is concentrated. In this case, it shows that most of the initial competition between those with different levels of education takes place in the secondary segment of the labour market, with a substantial proportion of such jobs now filled on a temporary basis by those with higher level qualifications. It is clear also that such temporary competition from the more highly qualified substantially increases the unemployment problems of those with poor qualifications. However, this kind of employer strategy may no longer be viable in a much tighter labour market.

(vi) Earnings

- Occupational status and education level achieved are both moderately to highly predictive of earnings; educational level continues to have positive effects despite controls for occupational status achieved and other relevant variables. There are, therefore, significant returns to increasing levels of education within most occupational categories.
- Besides these individual level effects, job/firm/industry characteristics also have substantial effects: the smaller the size of firm and the more it and jobs are located in the secondary segment of the labour market, the lower the earning rate. Also, entering and remaining in local, non-Dublin labour markets has a clear negative effect.
- Controlling for the above, being overqualified for one's (current) job has a clear negative effect on earnings. This is quite contrary to our hypothesis. Employers, therefore, appear to "distrust" the obviously overqualified who remain on in manual/service jobs. Perhaps those highly educated respondents who remain on in low status jobs are negatively selected on some unmeasured negative personal characteristics or work behaviours. Whatever the reason, there is no doubt from our data that they are not highly valued. Being underqualified for one's job has a clear negative earnings effect also, but this is as hypothesised.

CONCLUSIONS

One of the most pronounced characteristics of the Irish educational system, despite its obvious successes, is its inflexibility. Its full-time provision in rigidly timed sequences of instruction for most young people from four to 18, has little or no effective provision for those initially leaving the system having failed in it or being failed by it. There are almost no second chances given. Most of the limited flexibility present is in curricular/certification areas, rather than in instructional/course pacing, in part-time provision or in mixed education/training cumulative credit arrangements. Rigidities also in progression/access rules to further education limit access mainly to those who successfully complete the full-time system in general education, with few rewards for vocational/technical specialisation.

The recent reforms in the Scottish system (SOEID, 1994), the closest equivalent system in the EU, allow for much more flexibility and part-time and continuing education provision and much closer relationships between training and education.

These characteristics combined with three other characteristics of the relationship between educational qualifications and labour market outcomes create serious exclusionary pressures (though admittedly for a minority). These three characteristics are:

(i) The educational system has a high degree of standardisation and there is wide acceptance by employers of its qualifications as accurate measures of school/college leavers' educational performance and potential productivity. This effectively has come to mean that those with no or poor qualifications get no jobs or poor ones.

(ii) The predominance of the "general education" model, up to the completion of second level.

(iii) The relative unimportance of type of education — particularly vocational/technical — in employment decisions (Breen *et al.*, 1995; Breen and Whelan, 1998; Hannan and Ó Riain, 1993) also means that those with lower "academic abilities" — but perhaps with rich vocational technical aptitudes and other general aptitudes — are put at a serious disadvantage.

While Ireland is not a "credentialist country" (Müller and Karle, 1993; Shavit and Müller, 1998) in the same sense as is Germany or the Netherlands — where a clear connection between type of education and type of occupation taken up exists for a majority of entrants — there is a very close connection between level of education achieved, grades achieved in examinations and success in the labour market (Breen *et al.*, 1995). Using the concepts discussed in our first chapter, Ireland shows high rates of "level congruence" and low rates of "content congruence" in the education/labour-market relationship. This contrast sharply with "dual system" countries, such as the Netherlands or Germany, where the latter tends to be far more important — in apprenticeships, as well as in other routes into the labour market and further education and training.

The strength of the Irish system is this general educational "bias" and the high level and general nature of the human capital generated, guaranteeing a high level of flexibility amongst the younger workforce. This very general nature of human capital, however, also ensures high levels of competition between the more highly and the more poorly educated, even for low level jobs, particularly in times of high unemployment. This almost ensures the complete exclusion of a substantial proportion of the latter from the permanent workforce.

Given the strength and legitimacy of this educational tradition in Ireland and its undoubted advantages, but also the problems that almost inevitably flow from it, three policy conclusions appear justified:

a) We need to significantly expand the pre-school and early school interventions for our most deprived youth so as to reduce their level of educational failure, particularly at primary level. If the literacy and numeracy levels and general confidence about learning can be significantly improved amongst the bottom ten per cent of achievers leaving our primary school system, there should be a corresponding improvement in junior cycle performance.

b) We need to pay at least as much attention to increasing the flexibility and the pacing (mostly three years) of junior and senior cycle courses, as well as the number of subjects to be simultaneously taken at lower and upper second level, as we have paid so far to adjusting the curriculum and the examination system for "lower achievers". Diversifying the curriculum and examination system for the majority of lower achievers in a system that is so highly institutionalised, as has been our main policy so far, may not yield the best labour market outcomes for such lower conventional achievers — though it is certainly better than the alternative of having no qualifications.

c) Finally, we need to ensure that, at least within the educational and full-time training system itself, the currency of vocational technical subjects is fully recognised. Giving full credit for engineering, technology and other technical/vocational courses — by making them required subjects for access to relevant

> apprenticeships and third level courses, for instance — would be a major step forward. Being beaten for a relevant apprenticeship, third level course or job by somebody who has slightly more "points" than oneself, though in non-relevant general educational courses, is not designed to increase learning motivation for those taking such vocational/technical courses. Nor would it appear to increase the overall effectiveness of such education/training courses, or the quality of personal/educational "fit" to apprenticeships or relevant occupations.

At the time of this follow-up survey (1987–1992), when youth unemployment rates were much higher as a result of competition for even low level jobs, there was a significant overlap in the occupations entered by those with second and third level qualifications. This "overlap" declines over time, however. But even after an average of 2.5 years in the labour market, over 20 per cent of certificate, diploma and degree graduates were still in lower status manual/service occupations for which they were clearly overqualified. Some of this persistent "overqualification" is no doubt due to unobserved and negative personal characteristics of individuals; some to low productivity in first jobs; some to the willingness of some school/college leavers to take up and stay on in lower status jobs in their local labour market because they are willing to pay this price in order to stay on locally. In addition, some could be due to low performance in examinations — not measured in this data set for third level leavers. Also, given the high levels of youth unemployment, the substantial growth in educational levels amongst youth cohorts over the 1980s and early 1990s and the obvious willingness of a significant proportion of Irish youth to pay a price to stay at home rather than emigrate, one would have expected some degree of willingness to take up jobs of a lower status and earning rate than would be normally expected. In this context, and given the overall success of the Irish general educational model and the absence of any rules of correspondence in education/occupation matching in the Irish labour market, a figure of 20–25 per cent after two years does not appear to be too worrying. Nevertheless, some obvious overlaps in provision deserve policy attention.

From an educational provision point of view, the most policy-relevant overlap in provision occurs between some third level certificate courses and some Post Leaving Certificate (PLC) courses, particularly in non-Dublin labour markets. The main competition appears to occur between those with third level certificates and those with a Leaving Certificate (plus PLC) qualification, particularly in business studies courses. These PLC and third level graduates disproportionately enter clerical and lower administrative positions — mostly, it appears, in small firms (see Appendix Tables A4.2 to A4.4). Such occupations have generally poor career structures associated with them. The concentration of young women with such certificate qualifications in clerical occupations appears to be quite high (over one-third), with this percentage remaining relatively stable over time in the labour market. Although "level matched" in our definition, such a concentration of certificate graduates in clerical occupations — which is much more characteristic of those with a Leaving Certificate — clearly constrains their upward mobility chances. In addition, a higher percentage of female certificate respondents appear to be captured in lower skilled service occupations than is true of their male counterparts. Amongst males with certificate and diploma qualifications, upward career mobility into intermediate and higher technical occupations is more pronounced — partly explainable by the different types of technical qualifications originally specialised in.

The occupational overlap between those with a Leaving Certificate and those with such short-course third level qualifications, the high non-completion rate on these courses and the large areas of the country not directly served by these courses, indicate the need for significant rationalisation. Such further education and vocational/ technical training in local PLC courses for clerical/administrative positions would, for instance, be both more efficient and more linked to local labour market needs. Significant advances have already been made in improving the qualification framework for these courses through the NCVA. Given the obvious institutional lacuna in further and continuing education and training in Ireland and the relative absence of progression routes for those not going through the conventional full-time system, we would argue that it makes more sense to develop such further education and training, especially for intermediate level clerical/administrative positions, at PLC level.

The stability, if not continuing growth, of the new manufacturing sector, and the expansion of the service sector at increasing levels of sophistication, will require continuing expansion of a more highly educated/trained workforce, both for new youth entrants as well as for continuing education/training for adult workers. Strategically, the expansion of the "two and a half level" system would make more sense in the long term — given the apparent difficulty in restraining the continuing academic drift of the short-cycle third level system and the necessity to build a more flexible and locally/regionally adaptive continuing education/training system.

The rules of progression from one level to another within the Irish educational system, as well as between education, apprenticeship and work roles, are rarely based on "content congruence" in courses completed and courses/work applied for. Besides the obvious system inefficiencies involved, this creates a serious problem for the less academically able students. Those taking vocational/technical subjects at second level, for instance, are generally not given credit for this specialisation in applying for apprenticeships or further educational or vocational training courses. In particular, the use of "grade points" in selecting third level vocational/technical level courses — within the very restricted range of "points" involved — means both that those with slightly higher "points" in general educational courses are given preference over those with relevant vocational/technical qualifications, but slightly lower points. In a high proportion of such cases, those entering such further courses of study or apprenticeships have to "start from scratch" in the relevant study area. This is not only educationally inefficient but perhaps also partly explains the relatively high drop-out rate from some such third level courses.

The dominance of the "points race" (and "level congruence") in the Irish third level and labour market access system, while strengthening the growth of the general educational level of the workforce — and the motivation to learn of those in school — does have some serious consequences for school-goers who are not academically talented. At the same time, the vocational/technical weakness of many labour market entrants does not appear to be corrected by in-firm training programmes (O'Connell and Lyons, 1995). Indeed, unless such increased vocational/technical education and training is buttressed by the growth of such occupational entry prerequisites (i.e. by the expansion of the very small Irish "occupational labour market"), it is difficult to see how the current large flow into the labour market of "pass general" level students at

Leaving Certificate level can be improved upon. Evidence from previous analyses shows that such "pass general" (taking pass courses in general education rather than at honours levels or in vocational/technical courses) do not get on as well in the labour market as those with vocational/technical specialisations (Hannan and Ó Riain, 1993; Hannan and Shortall, 1991). The main effect of such vocational/technical specialisations — especially when linked successfully to labour market entry and subsequent vocational training arrangements — is not only to increase employment chances for the less academically inclined, but also to help workers move into skilled manual/technical occupations and avoid the more insecure and unskilled sectors of the labour market (Shavit and Müller, 1998).

Changes in the employment strategies of employers in the "secondary" services sector — retail/wholesale, hotels/restaurants, etc. — now appear essential. Up to the late 1990s, these have been able to select "off the top" of the queue of job applicants, and depend on the temporary employment of more highly educated school/college leavers to fill these posts. These employers are already feeling the pinch of a tightening labour market, with widespread reports of employers in the hotel and restaurant trade, for instance, recruiting from Spain. The high level of qualification inflation that occurred in such jobs since the early 1980s, with the easy availability of highly educated labour on a temporary basis, has meant little need for training and no appetite for the expansion of apprenticeships. Perhaps it is time for the state to become more active in both encouraging and rewarding employers in this sector in improving the education/training connection to good jobs in a situation of rapid growth and declining labour supply — especially with the rapid decline in cohort sizes from 1998 onwards. The proposed decline in company taxation can surely be linked to the need for more long-term planning and more training investment by this sector. A significant improvement in apprenticeship training in such services, linked with the current rapid growth in apprenticeships in construction and manufacturing, and in the context of the coming decline in youth cohort size, could provide a substantial impetus to rapid educational/training growth and employment rates amongst those from lower socio-economic backgrounds who make up the bulk of the more poorly qualified. The alternative of seeking more highly educated employees from abroad — which appears to be the strategy of some employers in the hotel and restaurant sector — both imposes its own costs on employers and would maintain high social costs on both the poorly educated and the society in general.

Given these current problems and continuing changes in the educational and training system, there is a need to go beyond current efforts and attempt to unify, or at least provide more "bridges" and mutually credited progression routes, between vocational education/ training and general education, and on to further and third level education. Ireland has extremely weak provision in all these respects. The extended comparative studies of Britain and Germany show, for instance, the strength of the German vocational training system and its positive effects on continuing education and training, as well as, more recently, in providing progression routes into further education and training. The British vocational training system provided little continuation education/training and is generally less standardised and integrated in its qualification structure (Heinz, 1992). In many respects, the Irish vocational training and further education system is even less satisfactory than the British one (O'Connell and Lyons, 1995) — with separate institutional provision, few operative qualification "bridges" between both systems, even if formal centralised qualification arrangements are now present. The more recent changes in Britain, and particularly in Scotland, provide a more unified education/training model towards which we should perhaps be moving: where all general and vocational curricular tracks and examinations are being brought into one unified framework and centralised institutional arrangements under one Ministry, with parity of esteem and progression to further education/training available to both tracks (SOEID, 1994).

In conclusion, therefore, given the strengths of the Irish system — particularly its general nature and high degree of acceptance/ institutionalisation by both parents/pupils and employers of its processes and outcomes — we can expect a relatively high level of labour market competition between school/college leavers to continue. We should try, however, to reduce its costs, both to the individuals and to society. Given future trends — such as continuing employment growth; declining numbers of school/college leavers; continuing upgrading of occupational levels by educational/training needs; less competition for jobs between people with different levels of education in the labour market, etc.; but also, continuing pressure for increasing the minimum level qualifications for a declining number of unskilled and semi-skilled manual and service jobs — the following policy objectives and changes appear desirable:

- A higher priority and greater provision to ensure a substantial reduction in the numbers failing in our current system — by setting more clear-cut targets, more resources and more ruthless targeting of these resources.
- Less attention to curricular/certification approaches toward reducing the "failure" levels, and more flexibility allowed in the pacing, number of subjects and subject combinations allowed at both junior and senior cycle levels. Using completely different types of curricula/examinations mainly for the least academically able students is not a strong selling point in the Irish labour market, and up to this point significantly restricts progression routes.
- Substantial expansion in the "two and a half" level system and rationalisation between it and short cycle third level courses. The necessity to both expand and target continuing education/training on local/regional labour market needs, combined with the variable regional coverage of, and apparent difficulty in restraining the academic drift in, short cycle third level provision, all argue for more strategic concentration on PLC level expansion in a restricted range of subjects.
- The very restricted nature of part-time, continuing education and training and the limited nature of in-firm training in Ireland — compared to our OECD equivalents — all argue also for the further development of continuing education and training and the greater integration of such provision and certification between education and training providers. Having two separate, and to some extent competitive, systems makes little sense in our very competitive environment.
- The very restricted extent to which courses taken in school are considered in determining access to further education or training courses — particularly vocationally oriented ones — introduces an over-academic bias in Irish selection mechanisms. A correction of this would not only increase the overall effectiveness of the

system, but would help to reduce the serious class inequalities present.

- The previous over-dependence of employers in the retail/wholesale, hotel and restaurant and other personal services sectors on "overqualified" temporary and part-time labour, and their apparent reluctance to invest in training, needs to be urgently addressed. This strategy is already threatened because of a tighter labour market but is likely to become even less viable as the number of school leavers start to decline rapidly from 1998 onwards. The replacement strategy of seeking more highly educated foreign workers will leave us with a persistent, serious unemployment problem for the least educationally qualified and leave them with few occupational goals to aim for. The rapid expansion of apprenticeships and traineeships in this sector seems essential. The proposed reduction in company taxation should perhaps be linked to persuading such employers to invest more in human capital rather than exploiting the surplus that has hitherto existed.

Appendix Tables

Table A4.1: Percentage Distribution of Male and Female Respondents at Work by Occupational Status (Hope-Goldthorpe Scale)

Hope-Goldthorpe Scale			**First Job**		**First Permanent Job**		**Current Job**	
No.	*Title*	*Scale Value*	*Male* %	*Female* %	*Male* %	*Female* %	*Male* %	*Female* %
1&2	Higher professionals — self-employed and salaried	71	6.0	3.1	7.0	3.5	8.4	4.4
3	High administrators and officials (higher grade)	69	0.7	0.1	0.7	0.3	1.6	0.9
4&5	Industrial managers — large enterprise; and administrators/officials	65	0.5	1.2	0.5	1.5	0.7	1.4
6	Technicians (higher grade)	63	2.0	1.7	2.2	2.5	3.0	2.7
8&9	Industrial and business managers (small enterprises)	62	2.9	7.3	3.6	9.3	6.2	13.9
10	Salaried professionals (lower grade)	61	0.9	–	0.7	0.2	1.1	0.4
11	Farmers and farm managers	58	0.3	–	0.3	–	0.6	0.1
12&13	Supervisors of non-manual employees (higher grade); and small proprietors	57	0.3	0.4	0.3	0.8	1.7	1.5
14	Managers in services and small administrative units	53	1.4	0.7	2.0	1.0	3.5	2.3
15	Technicians (lower grade)	51	0.5	0.3	0.6	0.5	1.1	0.6
16&17	Supervisors of lower non-manual and higher manual employees	47	–	0.1	0.2	0.3	1.1	0.6
18	Skilled manual workers in manufacturing (higher grade)	46	6.7	–	7.1	1.3	7.7	0.3
19&20	Self-employed workers (higher grade) and supervisors of manual employees (lower grade)	42	–	–	0.3	–	0.8	–
21	Non-manual employees in administration and commerce (e.g. clerical)	40	5.3	29.6	5.6	33.1	6.5	37.2
22&23	Skilled manual workers in manufacturing (intermediate) and construction	38	6.9	1.1	8.1	0.8	7.8	1.0

Hope-Goldthorpe Scale			**First Job**		**First Permanent Job**		**Current Job**	
No.	*Title*	*Scale Value*	*Male %*	*Female %*	*Male %*	*Female %*	*Male %*	*Female %*
24&25	Smallholders; and service workers (higher grade)	37	5.6	6.9	5.6	7.2	5.3	4.9
26&27	Semi-skilled manual workers in manufacturing; skilled manual workers in transport, communications and services	36	8.3	3.2	10.6	3.1	12.7	4.4
28&29	Service workers (intermediate grade); and self-employed service (intermediate grade) workers	35	8.7	15.8	8.3	11.8	3.8	7.7
30	Skilled manual workers in manufacturing (lower grade)	33	2.6	3.4	2.4	3.4	5.3	2.2
31	Agricultural workers	31	–	–	–	–	–	–
32	Semi-skilled manual workers in construction and extractive industries	30	7.0	0.2	6.1	0.1	5.0	0.2
33	Semi-skilled manual workers in transport, communications and services	28	2.9	2.4	2.9	2.2	3.6	2.0
34	Service workers (lower grade)	27	10.4	21.6	8.4	17.8	4.4	10.4
35	Unskilled manual and lower grade service workers	18	20.1	0.8	16.6	0.7	8.0	0.8
	Total N		*814*	*766*	*789*	*739*	*653*	*622*
	%		*100*	*100*	*100*	*100*	*100*	*100*
	Lower Interquartile Range		*27*	*30*	*27.3*	*35*	*33*	*36*
	Median		*35*	*37*	*36*	*40*	*38*	*40*
	Upper Interquartile Range		*40*	*40*	*46*	*40*	*53*	*57*
	SD		*15*	*12*	*15*	*12*	*15*	*13*
	Mean		*36*	*39*	*38*	*41*	*42*	*44*

Table A4.2: Percentage Distribution of Respondents at Work in First Job by Occupational Status and Educational Level

Hope-Goldthorpe Scale (First Job)			**Educational Level 1992**					
No.	*Title*	*Scale Value*	*No Quals %*	*Jun. Cert %*	*Leav. Cert %*	*Cert %*	*Dip. %*	*Deg. %*
1&2	Higher professionals — self-employed and salaried	71	–	–	0.9	13.4	15.0	21.4
3	High administrators and officials (higher grade)	69	–	–	0.1	0.7	1.2	2.3
4&5	Industrial managers — large enterprise; and administrators/officials	65	–	–	0.6	–	–	4.6
6	Technicians (higher grade)	63	–	–	0.2	7.7	15.1	4.9
8&9	Industrial and business managers (small enterprises)	62	–	–	4.1	3.7	3.8	22.7
10	Salaried professionals (lower grade)	61	–	–	0.4	1.6	–	1.1
11	Farmers and farm managers	58	–	–	0.3	–	–	–
12&13	Supervisors of non-manual employees (higher grade); and small proprietors	57	0.8	–	0.1	2.9	–	0.6
14	Managers in services & small administrative units	53	0.7	0.5	0.9	–	4.6	2.0
15	Technicians (lower grade)	51	–	–	0.6	0.7	1.8	–
16&17	Supervisors of lower non-manual and higher manual employees	47	–	–	–	–	1.5	–
18	Skilled manual workers in manufacturing (higher grade)	46	4.1	5.9	3.3	4.3	–	–
19&20	Self-employed workers (higher grade) and supervisors of manual employees (lower grade)	42	–	–	–	–	–	–
21	Non–manual employees in administration and commerce (e.g. clerical)	40	–	3.2	26.9	23.9	12.2	10.6
22&23	Skilled manual workers in manufacturing (intermediate) and construction	38	8.0	7.4	3.0	0.7	3.8	2.0

Hope-Goldthorpe Scale (First Job)			**Educational Level 1992**					
No.	*Title*	*Scale Value*	*No Quals %*	*Jun. Cert %*	*Leav. Cert %*	*Cert %*	*Dip. %*	*Deg. %*
24&25	Smallholders; and service workers (higher grade)	37	5.5	11.8	5.9	1.9	2.8	0.7
26&27	Semi-skilled manual workers in manufacturing; skilled manual workers in transport, communications and services	36	13.3	7.9	5.3	5.0	4.1	1.8
28&29	Service workers (intermediate grade); and self-employed service (intermediate grade) workers	35	10.7	13.8	14.0	7.9	5.0	7.5
30	Skilled manual workers in manufacturing (lower grade)	33	5.9	4.5	3.0	1.0	0.8	0.4
31	Agricultural workers	31	–	–	–	–	–	–
32	Semi-skilled manual workers in construction and extractive industries	30	6.1	6.2	3.3	2.6	–	1.2
33	Semi-skilled manual workers in transport, communications and services	28	5.1	4.2	2.7	0.7	–	0.5
34	Service workers (lower grade)	27	17.7	19.0	15.7	14.9	13.8	10.5
35	Unskilled manual and lower grade service workers	18	22.3	15.5	8.7	6.3	14.4	5.2
	Total N		*91*	*366*	*756*	*111*	*72*	*184*
	%		*100*	*100*	*100*	*100*	*100*	*100*
	Lower Interquartile Range		*27*	*27*	*28*	*32.3*	*27*	*35*
	Median		*30*	*35*	*36*	*40*	*40*	*62*
	Upper Interquartile Range		*36*	*37*	*40*	*62*	*63*	*65*
	SD		*8.4*	*7.7*	*10.4*	*16.2*	*18.5*	*17.5*
	Mean		*30.3*	*31.5*	*36*	*43.7*	*44.6*	*51.9*

Table A4.3: Percentage Distribution of Respondents at Work in First Permanent Job by Occupational Status and Educational Level

Hope-Goldthorpe Scale (First Permanent Job)			**Educational Level 1992**					
No.	*Title*	*Scale Value*	*No Quals %*	*Junior Cert %*	*Leav. Cert %*	*Cert %*	*Dip. %*	*Deg. %*
1&2	Higher professionals; self-employed and salaried	71	–	–	1.0	13.9	18.9	27.7
3	High administrators and officials (higher grade)	69	1.3	–	0.1	1.8	1.3	2.0
4&5	Industrial managers-large enterprise, and administrators/officials	65	–	–	0.8	0.7	–	5.0
6	Technicians (higher grade)	63	–	–	0.2	11.0	17.0	6.3
8&9	Industrial and business managers (small enterprises)	62	–	0.3	5.2	4.5	7.6	28.2
10	Salaried professionals (lower grade)	61	–	–	0.2	3.0	–	1.3
11	Farmers and farm managers	58	–	–	0.3	–	–	–
12&13	Supervisors of non-manual employees (higher grade); and small proprietors	57	1.8	–	0.4	3.7	–	–
14	Managers in services and small administrative units	53	0.8	–	1.6	0.7	7.4	3.1
15	Technicians (lower grade)	51	–	–	0.4	2.2	4.0	–
16&17	Supervisors of lower non-manual and higher manual employees	47	–	0.3	0.1	–	1.5	0.6
18	Skilled manual workers in manufacturing (higher grade)	46	4.7	5.3	3.8	4.3	0.7	–
19&20	Self-employed workers (higher grade); and supervisors of manual employees (lower grade)	42	–	0.4	0.1	–	–	–
21	Non-manual employees in administration and commerce (e.g. clerical)	40	–	4.6	30.2	22.7	9.9	9.2
22&23	Skilled manual workers in manufacturing (intermediate) and construction	38	9.8	8.1	3.9	0.7	1.3	1.2

Hope-Goldthorpe Scale (First Permanent Job)			**Educational Level 1992**					
No.	*Title*	*Scale Value*	*No Quals %*	*Junior Cert %*	*Leav. Cert %*	*Cert %*	*Dip. %*	*Deg. %*
24&25	Smallholders and service workers (higher grade)	37	5.1	11.6	6.1	2.8	3.0	0.8
26&27	Semi-skilled manual workers in manufacturing; skilled manual workers in transport, communications and services	36	14.2	9.5	7.0	4.2	5.5	0.7
28&29	Service workers (intermediate grade); and self-employed service (intermediate grade) workers	35	8.1	12.1	12.0	4.9	4.2	2.7
30	Skilled manual workers in manufacturing (lower grade)	33	8.7	4.9	2.3	1.0	0.9	0.5
31	Agricultural workers	31	–	–	–	–	–	–
32	Semi-skilled manual workers in construction and extractive industries	30	6.3	5.2	2.7	3.4	–	0.8
33	Semi-skilled manual workers in transport, communications and services	28	4.0	4.8	2.3	–	–	0.5
34	Service workers (lower grade)	27	15.8	20.0	11.6	11.5	5.1	6.8
35	Unskilled manual and lower grade service workers	18	19.4	13.0	7.8	2.8	11.8	2.5
	Total N		*81*	*356*	*745*	*110*	*69*	*167*
	%		*100*	*100*	*100*	*100*	*100*	*100*
	Lower Interquartile Range		*27*	*27*	*33*	*36*	*36*	*40*
	Median		*33*	*35*	*37*	*40*	*53*	*62*
	Upper Interquartile Range		*36*	*37*	*40*	*63*	*63*	*71*
	SD		*9.6*	*7.6*	*10.5*	*15.8*	*17.9*	*15.3*
	Mean		*31.7*	*32*	*37.3*	*47.4*	*49.5*	*57*

Table A4.4: Percentage Distribution of Respondents at Work in Current Job by Occupational Status and Educational Level

Hope-Goldthorpe Scale (Current Job)			**Educational Level 1992**					
No	*Title*	*Scale value*	*No Quals %*	*Jun. Cert %*	*Leav. Cert %*	*Cert %*	*Dip. %*	*Deg. %*
1&2	Higher professionals — self-employed and salaried	71	–	0.7	0.8	17.1	20.6	30.2
3	High administrators and officials (higher grade)	69	2.4	–	0.7	2.6	2.6	3.8
4&5	Industrial managers — large enterprise; and administrators/officials	65	–	–	0.8	–	–	5.2
6	Technicians (higher grade)	63	–	0.3	0.6	5.9	23.5	7.0
8&9	Industrial and business managers (small enterprises)	62	1.0	0.5	9.4	10.3	7.9	31.6
10	Salaried professionals (lower grade)	61	–	–	0.4	5.1	–	1.4
11	Farmers and farm managers	58	–	0.2	0.6	–	–	–
12&13	Supervisors of non-manual employees (higher grade); and small proprietors	57	1.7	1.7	1.6	5.1	–	–
14	Managers in services and small administrative units	53	–	1.9	3.1	2.3	11.6	1.6
15	Technicians (lower grade)	51	–	0.3	0.5	4.2	3.9	–
16&17	Supervisors of lower non-manual and higher manual employees	47	–	0.8	0.9	0.9	1.7	0.7
18	Skilled manual workers in manufacturing (higher grade)	46	7.6	4.7	5.0	2.8	1.3	–
19&20	Self-employed workers (higher grade) and supervisors of manual employees (lower grade)	42	1.1	0.7	0.4	0.5	–	–
21	Non-manual employees in administration and commerce (e.g. clerical)	40	–	7.2	33	24.8	4.5	6.5
22&23	Skilled manual workers in manufacturing (intermediate) and construction	38	7.3	10.4	3.9	–	1.3	0.7

Hope-Goldthorpe Scale (Current Job)			**Educational Level 1992**					
No	*Title*	*Scale value*	*No Quals %*	*Jun. Cert %*	*Leav. Cert %*	*Cert %*	*Dip. %*	*Deg. %*
24&25	Smallholders and service workers (higher grade)	37	6.1	10.3	4.5	5.4	0.7	0.5
26&27	Semi-skilled manual workers in manufacturing; skilled manual workers in transport, communications and services	36	16.0	15.5	8.2	3.1	9.2	–
28&29	Service workers (intermediate grade); and self-employed service (intermediate grade) workers	35	12.0	5.9	7.3	–	–	2.5
30	Skilled manual workers in manufacturing (lower grade)	33	14.3	8.5	2.7	1.1	1.3	0.5
31	Agricultural workers	31	–	–	–	–	–	–
32	Semi-skilled manual workers in construction and extractive industries	30	1.9	5.3	2.8	0.8	1.2	–
33	Semi-skilled manual workers in transport, communications and services	28	6.6	5.6	2.4	–	1.9	1.0
34	Service workers (lower grade)	27	3.9	11.0	7.0	5.8	6.8	4.8
35	Unskilled manual and lower grade service workers	18	18.1	8.6	3.4	2.1	–	2.0
	Total N		*43*	*258*	*662*	*98*	*63*	*152*
	%		*100*	*100*	*100*	*100*	*100*	*100*
	Lower Interquartile Range		*28*	*28*	*35*	*40*	*40*	*62*
	Median		*35*	*36*	*40*	*51*	*62*	*62*
	Upper Interquartile Range		*37*	*38*	*40*	*63*	*63*	*71*
	SD		*10.7*	*8.8*	*11.1*	*14.8*	*14.6*	*13.9*
	Mean		*33.6*	*34.8*	*40.8*	*51*	*54.7*	*59.5*

Table A4.5: Average and Standard Deviation, Occupational Status Values (Hope-Goldthorpe 1974 scale, for first job, first permanent job and current job for all labour market entrants, by level of education, 1992)

	Level of Education					
				Third Level		
	No Quals	*JC Quals*	*LC Quals*	*Certificate*	*Diploma*	*Degree*
1. First Job						
Average	30	32	36	44	45	52
(SD)	(8)	(8)	(10)	(16)	(19)	(18)
N	91	366	756	111	72	184
2. First Permanent Job						
Average	32	32	37	47	50	57
(SD)	(9)	(8)	(11)	(16)	(18)	(15)
N	81	556	745	110	69	167
3. Current Job						
Average	34	35	41	51	55	60
(SD)	(11)	(9)	(11)	(15)	(15)	(14)
N	43	258	662	78	63	152

Table A5.1: Percentage of Respondents "Overqualified" in First Permanent Job by Level of Education and Type of Education (vocational vs. other)

	Level of Education			
	Junior Cert. or Less	*Leaving Cert.*	*Third Level Cert. or Diploma*	*University Degree*
*I: Vocational Technical Qualifications at Second Level**	*% Overqualified*			
1. With Vocational Technical Subjects	0	38% (159)	41% (39)	15% (26)
2. Without	0	23% (604)	25% (149)	21% (188)
*II: Professional Technical Qualifications at Third Level***	*% Overqualified*			
1. With Professional Technical Qualifications	–	–	25% (76)	18% (74)
2. Without	–	–	28% (94)	21% (138)

* Vocational-Technical Subjects include Woodwork, Metalwork, Technical Drawing at lower second level and Engineering, Construction Studies at upper second level

** Professional-Technical qualifications include Medicine, Law, Engineering, Computer Science, etc.

Table A5.2: Percentage of Respondents "Overqualified" in Current Job by Level of Education and Vocational, Technical-Professional Qualification

	Level of Education			
	Junior Cert. or Less	*Leaving Cert.*	*Third Level Cert. or Diploma*	*University Degree*
*I: Vocational Technical Qualifications at Second Level**	*% Overqualified*			
1. With Vocational Technical Subjects	– (185)	26% (159)	31% (39)	8% (26)
2. Without	– (308)	13% (604)	13% (149)	14% (188)
*II: Professional Technical Qualifications at Third Level***	*% Overqualified*			
1. With Professional Technical Qualifications	–	–	9% (76)	11% (74)
2. Without	–	–	20% (94)	14% (138)

* Vocational-Technical Subjects include Woodwork, Metalwork, Technical Drawing at lower second level and Engineering, Construction Studies at upper second level.

** Professional-Technical qualifications include Medicine, Law, Engineering, Computer Science, etc.

Table A5.3: Effects of Socio-Economic Background Factors, Educational Achievement Level, Type of Education (number of vocational technical subjects and whether qualified at third level in professional/technical area), Occupational Status of First Permanent Job as well as Other Variables on Current Occupational Status (Multiple Regression (OLS))

Independent Variable	**Occupational Status (Hope-Goldthorpe) of Current Job**
	β
1. Father's Occupational Status	.02
2. Father Unemployed (= 1, other = 0)	.61
3. Mother's Educational Level	.59
4. Number of Children in Family	.11
5. Gender (female = 1, male = 0)	–1.09
6. From West Origin	–.65
7. Level of Educational Attainment	.71**
7a. Number of Vocational-Technical Subjects at Second Level	–.98**
7b. With Professional/Technical Qualifications	3.75**
8. Occupational Status for First Permanent Job	.62**
9. Overeducated for First Permanent Job	3.73**
10. Local Non-Dublin Labour Market	–1.11
11. Emigrant	.32
R^2	*.56*
df	*13/1136*
p	*<.001*

Table A6.1: Industry of First Job by Level of Education

Industry	No Quals	Group Cert	Inter Cert	Inter Cert+*	Leaving Cert	Cert/Dip	Degree	Total
	Per Cent							
1. Agricultural/Fishing	12.9	13.3	8.1	12.8	6.4	5.4	1.4	7.0
2. Manufacturing	32.7	25.4	20.9	27.7	17.6	16.6	18.5	19.7
3. Construction	9.4	10.0	11.0	9.2	5.9	11.2	4.1	7.6
4. Retail/Wholesale	19.6	25.0	25.2	24.3	25.3	13.6	13.6	22.2
5. Personal Services	20.8	19.5	25.9	14.3	15.1	15.0	8.8	16.4
6. Professional Services	–	1.9	2.7	9.7	13.5	16.3	37.6	13.6
7. Banking/Insurance	–	1.2	2.7	–	7.7	7.9	7.4	5.9
8. Others	4.6	3.6	3.5	1.8	8.3	14.0	8.5	7.6
Total %	*5.8*	*5.3*	*13.6*	*4.0*	*47.7*	*11.7*	*11.7*	*100*
N	*92*	*84*	*216*	*65*	*755*	*185*	*185*	*1582*

* "Inter Cert +" refers to those who participated in VPT1 courses.

Table A6.2: Industry of First Permanent Job by Level of Education

Industry	No Quals	Group Cert	Inter Cert	Inter Cert+	Leaving Cert	Cert/Dip	Degree	Total
	Per Cent							
1. Agricultural/Fishing	13.0	13.0	6.1	11.4	6.0	5.3	0.8	6.4
2. Manufacturing	33.2	27.1	23.5	30.8	18.3	20.5	20.9	21.3
3. Construction	10.7	11.7	9.2	11.2	6.0	9.2	3.9	7.4
4. Retail/Wholesale	15.3	19.2	22.8	18.7	25.0	8.5	7.4	19.8
5. Personal Services	21.3	20.3	26.1	14.9	13.8	13.7	6.6	15.5
6. Professional Services	–	2.5	5.0	10.1	13.3	20.7	43.1	14.9
7. Banking/Insurance	–	2.5	3.5	–	73.8	9.2	10.1	6.6
8. Others	6.4	3.8	3.8	3.0	9.6	13.0	7.2	8.2
Total %	*5.4*	*5.3*	*13.8*	*4.2*	*48.7*	*11.7*	*10.7*	*100*
N	*83*	*81*	*211*	*64*	*744*	*179*	*167*	*1528*

Table A6.3: Industry of Current Job by Level of Education

Industry	No Quals	Group Cert	Inter Cert	Inter Cert+	Leaving Cert	Cert/Dip	Degree	Total
	Per Cent							
1. Agricultural/Fishing	8.9	7.9	7.3	13.2	5.1	3.6	0.9	5.2
2. Manufacturing	29.8	38.9	22.3	47.3	23.4	25.4	21.8	25.0
3. Construction	20.6	16.0	17.3	6.5	5.6	7.3	1.4	7.8
4. Retail/Wholesale	21.3	13.5	16.8	14.2	20.5	7.2	4.5	16.0
5. Personal Services	6.1	6.9	19.3	7.4	8.8	11.2	6.4	9.9
6. Professional Services	–	1.8	2.3	–	12.3	17.7	47.7	14.7
7. Banking/Insurance	–	1.8	0.9	1.8	9.2	9.0	9.8	7.4
8. Others	13.2	13.2	13.8	9.5	15.1	18.7	7.6	14.2
Total %	*3.4*	*4.4*	*12.4*	*3.3*	*51.7*	*12.9*	*11.9*	*100*
N	*44*	*57*	*159*	*43*	*662*	*165*	*152*	*1280*

Table A6.4: Relationship between Categorisations of Occupations (and Industries) for Hope-Goldthorpe Scale and of Sectoral Allocation (median occupational status and upper and lower interquartile ranges for each sector)

Hope-Goldthorpe (Occupational Status) Scale (values 17–72)	**Sectoral Category**			
	Independent Primary: Professional	*Independent Primary: Craft*	*Subordinate Primary*	*Secondary*
Median Status Value	63.2	38.3	37.8	34.9
Upper IQ Range:	70.3	46.0	39.8	39.8
Lower IQ Range	53.1	37.5	36.2	27.3

Table A6.5: Percentage Currently Employed in Secondary Sector by Level of Education; and Percentage "Overqualified" by Level of Education and Sector

	Level of Education				
	No Quals	*Junior Cert*	*Leaving Cert*	*Third Level Cert/Dip*	*Univ. Degree*
1. Percentage of those currently employed in secondary sector	52% (43)	44% (256)	41% (658)	25% (163)	13% (152)
2. Of those in different sectors:	*Percentage Overqualified*				
(a) Primary Professional	*	0	11%	0%	0%
(b) Primary: Craft	*	0%	2%	20%	*
(c) Subordinate Primary	0%	0%	10%	15%	0%
(d) Secondary	0%	0%	31%	54%	86%

* N < 10

Bibliography

Allmendinger, J. (1989), "Educational Systems and Labour Market Outcomes", *European Sociological Review*, Vol. 5, No. 3, pp. 213–250.

Anisef, P., F. Ashbury, A.H. Turrittin and N. Guppy (1992), "Differential Effects of University and Community College Education on Occupational Status Attainment in Ontario", *Canadian Journal of Sociology*, Vol. 17, No. 1, pp. 69–84.

Ashenfelter, O. and J.D. Mooney (1968), "Graduate Education, Ability and Earnings", *Review of Economics and Statistics*, Vol. 50, February, pp. 78–86.

Arrow, K. (1973), "Higher Education as a Filter", *Journal of Public Economics*, Vol. 2, pp. 193–216.

Ashton, D., F. Green and G. Lowe (1993), "The Linkages Between Education and Employment in Canada and the UK: A Comparative Analysis", *Comparative Education*, Vol. 29, No. 2, pp. 125–144.

Ashton, D. and G. Lowe (eds.) (1991), *Making their Way: Education, Training and the Labour Market in Canada and Britain*, Milton Keynes: Open University Press.

Ashton, D., M. Maguire and M. Spilsbury (1990), *Restructuring the Labour Market: The Implications for Youth*, London: Macmillan.

Ashton, D. and J. Sung (1992), "The Determinants of Labour Market Transitions: An Exploration of Contrasting Approaches", *Work, Employment and Society*, Vol. 6, No. 1, pp. 1–21.

Barrett, A., T. Callan and B. Nolan (1997), "The Earnings Distribution and Returns to Education in Ireland 1987–1994", CEPR Discussion Paper No. 1679, London: Centre for Economic Policy Research.

Bates, I. and G. Riseborough (1993), *Youth and Inequality*, London: Open University Press.

Becker, G. (1964), *Human Capital*, New York: National Bureau of Economic Research (NBER).

Beduwé, C. and P. Robinson (1996), "Diplômes, Compétences et Marchés du Travail en Europe", Strasbourg: Economic Science Foundation, Working Paper.

Berg, I. (1970), *Education and Jobs: The Great Training Robbery*, New York: Praeger Publishers.

Bidwell, C. (1989), "The Meaning of Educational Attainment", *Research in the Sociology of Education and Socialisation*, Vol. 8, pp. 117–138.

Bills, D.B. (1988a), "Educational Credentials and Hiring Decisions: What Employers Look for in Entry Level Employees", *Research in Social Stratification and Mobility*, Vol. 7, pp. 71–97.

Bills, D.B. (1988b), "Educational Credentials and Promotions: Does Schooling do More than Get you in the Door?", *Sociology of Education*, Vol. 61, pp. 52–60.

Bills, D.B. (1992), "The Mutability of Educational Credentials as Hiring Criteria". *Work and Occupations*. Vol. 19, No. 1, pp. 79–95.

Blackaby, D., K. Clarke and D. Leslie (1995), "Dual Labour Markets and the Potential Earnings of the Unemployed", *Scottish Journal of Political Economy*, Vol. 42, No. 1, pp. 37–52.

Blau, P. and O.D. Duncan (1967), *The American Occupational Structure*, New York: John Wiley and Sons.

Blaug, M.B. (1967), "The Private and the Social Returns on Investment in Education: Some Results for Great Britain", *Journal of Human Resources*, Vol. 2, Summer, pp. 330–346.

Bowles, S. and H. Gintis (1976), *Schooling in Capitalist America*, New York: Basic Books.

Boylan, R.D. and J.P. Morgan (1993), "The Effect of the Number of Diplomas on their Value", *Sociology of Education*, Vol. 66, No. 3, pp. 206–221.

Bradley, S. and T. Taylor (1996), "Human Capital Formation and Location Economic Performance", *Regional Studies*, Vol. 30, No. 1, pp. 1–14.

Breen, R. (1984a), *Education and the Labour Market: Work and Unemployment among Recent Cohorts of Irish School Leavers*, ESRI General Research Series No. 119, Dublin: The Economic and Social Research Institute.

Breen, R. (1984b), "Status Attainment or Job Attainment? The Effects of Sex and Class on Youth Unemployment", *British Journal of Sociology*, Vol. 35, No. 3, pp. 363–386.

Breen, R. (1995), "The Persistence of Class Origin Inequalities among School Leavers in the Republic of Ireland, 1984–1993", European Science Foundation Working Paper.

Breen, R., D.F. Hannan and R. O'Leary (1995), "Returns to Education: Taking Account of Employers' Perceptions and Use of Educational Credentials", *European Sociological Review*, Vol. 11, No. 1, May, pp. 59–73.

Breen, R. and C.T. Whelan (1996), *Social Mobility and Social Class in Ireland*, Dublin: Gill and Macmillan.

Breen, R. and C.T. Whelan (1998), "Investment in Education: Educational Qualifications and Class of Entry in the Republic of Ireland" in Y. Shavit and M. Müller (eds.), *From School to Work*, Oxford: Clarendon.

Breneman, D. and S. Nelson (1981), *Financing Community Colleges: An Economic Perspective*, Washington DC: The Brookings Institute.

Brown, P. (1995), "Cultural Capital and Social Exclusion: Some Observations on Recent Trends in Education, Employment and the Labour Market", *Work, Employment and Society*, Vol. 9, No. 1, pp. 29–51.

Burris, V. (1983), "The Social and Political Consequences of Overeducation", *American Sociological Review*, Vol. 48, pp. 454–467.

Bynner, J. (1996), "Skills as Human Capital in Youth Transitions", Strasbourg: European Science Foundation, Working Paper.

Callan, T. and C. Harmon (1997), "The Economic Return to Schooling in Ireland", UCD Centre for Economic Research WP 92/23, Dublin: UCD Department of Economics.

Callan, T. and B. Nolan (1993), "Income Inequality and Poverty in Ireland in the 1970s and 1980s", ESRI Working Paper No. 43, Dublin: The Economic and Social Research Institute.

Callan, T. and A. Wren (1994), *Male-Female Wage Differentials: Analysis and Policy Issues,* ESRI General Research Series Paper No. 163, Dublin: The Economic and Social Research Institute.

Canny, A., G. Hughes and J.J. Sexton (1995), *Occupational Employment Forecasts 1998,* FÁS/ESRI Manpower Forecasting Studies, Report No. 4. Dublin: FÁS/ESRI.

Casey, B. (1986), "The Dual Apprenticeship System and the Recruitment and Retention of Young Persons in West Germany", *British Journal of Industrial Relations,* Vol. 24, pp. 63–82.

CEDEFOP (1991), "Qualifications for a Changing World", *Vocational Training,* 2/1991.

Clogg, C. and J.W. Shockey (1984), "Mismatch Between Occupation and Schooling: A Prevalence Measure — Recent Trends and Demographic Analysis", *Demography,* Vol. 21, pp. 235–257.

Collins, R. (1979), *The Credential Society,* New York: Academic Press.

Cregan, C. (1991), "Young Workers and the Job-swapping Phenomenon", *Work, Employment and Society,* Vol. 5, No. 3, pp. 417–436.

Dex, S. (1982), *Black and White School Leavers: The First Five Years of Work,* London: Dept. of Employment, Research Paper No. 33.

Dickens, W.T. and K. Lang (1985), "A Test of Dual Labor Market Theory", *American Economic Review,* Vol. 75, No. 4.

Dickens, W.T. and K. Lang (1993), "Labour Market Segmentation Theory: Reconsidering the Evidence" in W. Darity Jr. (ed.), *Labor Economics: Problems in Analyzing Labor Markets,* Boston/Dordrecht: Kluwer.

Doeringer, P. and M. Piore (1971), *Internal Labor Markets and Manpower Analysis*, Massachusetts: Heath Lexington Books.

Dore, R. (1976), *The Diploma Disease*, London: George Allen and Unwin Ltd.

Dougherty, K. (1987), "The Effects of Community Colleges: Aid or Hindrance to Socio-economic Attainment?", *Sociology of Education*, Vol. 60, pp. 86–103.

Duggan, D., G. Hughes and J.J. Sexton (1997), *Occupational Employment Forecasts 2003*, FÁS/ESRI Manpower Forecasting Studies, Report No. 6, Dublin: FÁS/ESRI.

Duncan, O.D. and J.W. Artis (1951), *Social Stratification in a Pennsylvania Rural Community*, Pennsylvania State College, Agricultural Experiment Station Bulletin 543.

Duncan, O.D. and B. Duncan (1955), "A Methodological Analysis of Segregation Indices", *American Sociological Review*, Vol. 20.

Duncan, O.D., D. Featherman and B. Duncan (1972), *Socioeconomic Background and Achievements*, New York: Seminar Press.

Duncan, G.J. and S.D. Hoffman (1981), "The Incidence and Wage Effects of Overeducation", *Economics of Education Review*, Vol. 1, pp. 57–86.

Erikson, R. and J. Goldthorpe (1992), *The Constant Flux: A Study of Class Mobility in Industrial Societies*, Oxford: Clarendon Press.

Freeman, R. (1976), *The Overeducated American*, New York: Academic Press.

Gordon, D. (1986), *Procedure for Allocating Jobs into Labor Segments*, New School for Social Research (mimeo.).

Gordon, D., R. Edwards and M. Reich (1982), *Segmented Work, Divided Workers: The Historical Transformation of Labor in the United States*, Cambridge: Cambridge University Press.

Grendon, B. (1996), *L'evolution de la transition de l'école vers la vie active en France*, Report prepared for the OECD.

Griffin, L., A. Kallenberg and K.L. Alexander (1981), "Determinants of Early Labour Market Entry and Attainment: A Study of Labour Market Segmentation", *Sociology of Education*, Vol. 54, pp. 205–221.

Grubb, W.N. (1995), "The Varied Economic Returns to Post-secondary Education: New Evidence from the Class of 1972: Response", *Journal of Human Resources*, Vol. 30, No. 1, pp. 222–228.

Hannan, D.F. (1970), *Rural Exodus: A Study of the Forces Influencing the Large-Scale Migration of Irish Rural Youth*, Dublin: Geoffrey Chapman.

Hannan, D.F. (1986), *Schooling and the Labour Market*, Shannon: Shannon CDU and Department of Education.

Hannan, D.F. (1992), "Education Employment and Local Economic Development" in J.P. Davis (ed.), *Education Training and Local Economic Development*, Dublin: Regional Studies Association.

Hannan, D.F. (1996), "School to Work and Adulthood Transitions in Ireland: Problems and Possibilities", Paper presented at the National Economic and Social Forum, 16 January, Dublin.

Hannan, D.F. and S. McCoy (1995), "Early School Leavers: Reform of the Junior Certificate, Educational Achievement and Employment Chances", ESRI Working Paper No. 67.

Hannan, D.F. and S. Ó Riain (1993), *Pathways to Adulthood in Ireland: Causes and Consequences of Success and Failure in Transitions amongst Irish Youth*, ESRI General Research Series Paper No. 161, Dublin: The Economic and Social Research Institute.

Hannan, D.F., D. Raffe and E. Smyth, OECD (1996), "Cross-National Research on School to Work Transitions: An Analytical Framework", Background Paper to OECD.

Hannan, D.F. and S. Shortall (1991), *The Quality of their Education: School Leavers' Views of Educational Objectives and Outcomes*, ESRI General Research Series Paper No. 153, Dublin: The Economic and Social Research Institute.

Hannan, D.F. and E. Smyth (1994), "Qualification Inflation and Mobility Within the Youth Labour Market", ESRI Unpublished Seminar Paper.

Hannan, D.F. and E. Smyth (1995), "1985/86 School Leavers: A Follow-up Study in 1992", ESRI Working Paper No. 65.

Harmon, C. and I. Walker (1995), "Estimates of the Economic Return to Schooling for the UK", Institute for Fiscal Studies/ESRC Working Paper No. W95/12.

Hartog, J. and H. Oosterbeek (1988), "Education, Allocation and Earnings in the Netherlands: Overschooling?", *Economics of Education Review*, Vol. 7, No. 2, pp. 185–194.

Hecker, D. (1992), "Reconciling Conflicting Data on Jobs for College Graduates", *Monthly Labour Review*, July, pp. 3–12.

Heinz, W. (1992), "Access to Working Life in Germany and Britain" in A. Cavalli and O. Galland, *Youth in Europe*, London: Pinter.

Hope, K. and J. Goldthorpe (1974), *The Social Grading of Occupations: A New Approach and Scale*, Oxford: Clarendon Press.

Hughes, G. and B. Nolan (1997), "Segmented Labour Markets and Earnings in Ireland", *The Economic and Social Review*, Vol. 28, No. 1, pp. 1–22.

Hunter, A. (1988), "Formal Education and Initial Employment: Unraveling the Relationships Between Schooling and Skills Over Time", *American Sociological Review*, Vol. 53, pp. 753–765.

Hunter, A. (1993), "On Formal Education, Skills and Earnings: The Role of Educational Certificates in Earnings Determination", *Canadian Journal of Sociology*, Vol. 18, No. 1, pp. 21–42.

Johnson, W.R. (1978), "A Theory of Job Shopping", *Quarterly Journal of Economics*, May, pp. 261–278.

Jones, P. (1985), "Qualifications and Labour Market Outcomes Among 16-Year-Old School Leavers", *British Journal of Guidance and Counselling*, Vol. 13, No. 3, pp. 275–291.

Jovanovic, B. (1979), "Job Matching and the Theory of Turnover", *Journal of Political Economy*, Vol. 87, October, pp. 972–90.

Karabel, J. (1972), "Community Colleges and Social Stratification", *Harvard Education Review*, Vol. 42, pp. 521–562.

Kerckhoff, A. (1993), *Diverging Pathways: Social Structure and Career Deflections*, Cambridge: Cambridge University Press.

Kerckhoff, A., R. Campbell and J. Trott (1982), "Dimensions of Educational and Occupational Attainment in Great Britain", *American Sociological Review*, Vol. 47, June, pp. 347–364.

Kroch, E.A. and K. Sjoblom (1994), "Schooling as Human Capital or a Signal: Some Evidence", *Journal of Human Resources*, Vol. 29, pp. 156–180.

Layard, R. and G. Psacharopoulos (1974), "The Screening Hypothesis and the Returns to Education", *Journal of Political Economy*, Vol. 82, No. 5, pp. 985–998.

McGrath, J. (1995), "The Qualifications of the Irish Workforce", *Labour Market Review*, Vol. 5, No. 2, pp. 1–17.

McNabb, R. and P. Ryan (1990), "Segmented Labour Markets" in D. Sapsford and Z. Tzannatos (eds.), *Current Issues in Labour Economics*, London: Macmillan.

Mathiesan, A. (1980), "Polarisation of the Qualification Structure of the Danish Labour Force: The Role of the Educational System in Post-war Denmark", *Acta Sociologica*, Vol. 23, Nos. 2–3, pp. 157–172.

Medsker, L. (1960), *The Junior College*, New York: McGraw-Hill.

Monk-Turner, E. (1988), "Educational Differentiation and Status Attainments: The Community College Controversy", *Sociological Focus*, Vol. 21, No. 2, pp. 141–151.

Monk-Turner, E. and Y. Baba (1987), "Gender and College Opportunities: Changes Over Time in the US and Japan", *Sociological Inquiry*, Vol. 57, No. 3, pp. 292–303.

Müller, W. and W. Karle (1993), "Social Selection in Educational Systems in Europe", *European Sociological Review*, Vol. 9, No. 1, pp. 1–23.

Müller, W., Y. Shavit and P. Ucen (1996), "The Institutional Embeddedness of the Stratification Process: A Comparative Study of Qualifications and Occupations in Thirteen Countries", Strasbourg: European Science Foundation, Working Paper.

Nakajima, F. (1990), "Comparative Study on Choice of First Job and Early Occupation: History in Japan, the US and GB", Tokyo: The Japanese Institute of Labour, Working Paper.

NESC (1991), "The Economic and Social Implications of Emigration", NESC Report No. 90, Dublin: National Economic and Social Council.

NESF (1997), "Early School Leavers and Youth Unemployment", NESF Report No. 11, Dublin: National Economic and Social Forum.

Nutter, R.W. and M. Zapf (1990), "Comparisons among Community College Graduates, University Transfer and After-Degree Students in a BSW Program: Is Where They Come from Important?" *Canadian Social Work Review*, Vol. 7, No. 2, pp. 260–272.

O'Connell, P. and M. Lyons (1995), *Enterprise-Related Training and State Policy in Ireland: The Training Support Scheme*, ESRI Policy Research Series No. 25, Dublin: The Economic and Social Research Institute.

OECD (1995), *Education at a Glance*, Paris: Organisation for Economic Co-operation and Development.

OECD (1996a), *Education at a Glance*, Paris: Organisation for Economic Co-operation and Development.

OECD (1996b), *Employment Outlook*, Paris: Organisation for Economic Co-operation and Development.

Osterman, P. (1980), "An Empirical Study of Labor Market Segmentation", *Industrial and Labor Relations Review*, Vol. 28, pp. 508–523.

Payne, G. (1987), *Employment and Opportunity*, London: Macmillan.

Payne, J. and C. Payne (1985), *Youth Unemployment 1974–1981: The Changing Importance of Age and Qualification*, London: Economic and Social Research Council.

Psacharopoulos, G. (1993), "Returns to Investments in Education: A Global Update", World Bank Working Paper, No. 1067.

Raffe, D. (ed.) (1984), *Fourteen to Eighteen*, Aberdeen: Aberdeen University Press.

Robst, J. (1995), "Career Mobility, Job Match, and Overeducation", *Eastern Economic Journal*, Vol. 21, No. 4, pp. 539–550.

Rosenbaum, J.E. and T. Kariya (1991), "Do School Achievements Affect the Early Jobs of High School Graduates in the United States and Japan?" *Sociology of Education*, Vol. 64, No. 2, pp. 78–95.

Rosenthan, N. (1995), "The Nature of Occupational Employment Growth: 1983–93", *Monthly Labour Review*, Vol. 118, No. 6, pp. 45–54.

Rumberger, R.W. (1981a), "The Rising Incidence of Overeducation in the US Labor Market", *Economics of Education Review*, Vol. 1, No. 3, pp. 293–314.

Rumberger, R.W. (1981b), "The Impact of Surplus Schooling on Productivity and Earnings", *The Journal of Human Resources*, Vol. 22, No. 1, pp. 24–50.

Schupp, J., C.F. Büchtemann and D. Soloff (1994), "School to Work Transition Patterns in (West) Germany and the United States", Strasbourg: European Science Foundation, Working Paper.

Schultz, T.W. (1961), "Education and Economic Growth" in N. Henry (ed.), *Social Forces Influencing American Education*, Chicago: University of Chicago Press.

Schultz, T.W. (1963), *The Economic Value of Education*, New York: Columbia University Press.

Schultz, T.W. (1971), *Investment in Human Capital*, New York: The Free Press.

Sewell, W. and R. Hauser (1975), *Education, Occupation and Earnings: Achievement in the Early Career*, New York: Academic Press.

Sexton, J.J., A. Canny and G. Hughes (1996), *Changing Profiles in Occupations and Educational Attainment*, FÁS/ESRI Manpower Forecasting Studies Report No. 5, Dublin: FÁS/ESRI.

Sexton, J.J., B. Walsh, D.F. Hannan, and D. McMahon (1991), *The Economic and Social Implications of Emigration*, Dublin: National Economic and Social Council.

Shavit, Y. and M. Müller (1998), *From School to Work*, Oxford: Clarendon.

Shockey, J.W. (1989), "Overeducation and Earnings: A Structural Approach to Differential Attainment in the United States Labor Force (1970–82)", *American Sociological Review*, Vol. 54, pp. 856–864.

Sicherman, N. (1991), "Overeducation in the Labour Market", *Journal of Labour Economics*, Vol. 9, No. 2, pp. 101–122.

Sly, F. (1993), "Economic Activity of 16 and 17 Year Olds", *Employment Gazette*, July 1993, pp. 307–312.

Smart, J. (1988), "College Influences on Graduates' Income Levels", *Research in Higher Education*, Vol. 28, No. 1, pp. 41–59.

Smith, H. (1986), "Overeducation and Underemployment: An Agnostic Review", *Sociology of Education*, Vol. 59, pp. 85–99.

Smyth, E. (1997), "Labour Market Structures and Women's Employment in Ireland" in M. Leonard and A. Byrne (eds.), *Women in Ireland: A Sociological Perspective*, Belfast: Beyond the Pale.

Smyth, E. and P. Surridge (1995), "A Comparative Analysis of School to Work Transition Patterns and Processes in Ireland and Scotland, 1979–1991", Strasbourg: European Science Foundation, Working Paper.

Smyth, E. and P. Surridge (1996), "Educational Differences and Occupational Allocation among School Leavers in Ireland and Scotland, 1981–1991", Strasbourg: European Science Foundation, Working Paper.

SOEID (1994), *Higher Still: Opportunity for All*, Edinburgh: SOEID.

Spence, A. (1974), *Market Signalling: Information Transfer in Hiring and Related Processes*, Cambridge, MA: Harvard University Press.

Spence, M. (1973), "Job Market Signalling", *Quarterly Journal of Economics*, Vol. 87, pp. 353–374.

Spilerman, S. (1977), "Careers, Labor Market Structure, and Socio-economic Achievement", *American Journal of Sociology*, Vol. 83, No. 3, pp. 551–593.

Spilerman, S. (1986), "Organizational Rules and the Features of Work Careers" in D. Treiman and R. Robinson (eds.), *Research in Social Stratification and Mobility*, Greenwich: JAI.

Spilerman, S. and T. Lunde (1991), "Features of Educational Attainment and Job Promotion Prospects", *American Journal of Sociology*, Vol. 97, pp. 689–720.

Stiglitz, J. (1975), "The Theory of 'Screening', Education and the Distribution of Income", *American Economic Review*, Vol. 65, pp. 283–300.

Thurow, L. (1975), *Generating Inequality*, New York: Basic Books.

Tyler, J., R. Murnane and F. Levy (1995), "Are More College Graduates Really Taking 'High School' Jobs?", *Monthly Labour Review*, Vol. 118, No. 2, pp. 18–27.

Tzanatos, Z. (1990), "Employment Segregation: Can We Measure It and What Does the Measure Mean?", *British Journal of Industrial Relations*, Vol. 28, No. 1, March, pp. 105–111.

Velez, W. (1985), "Finishing College: The Effects of College Type", *Sociology of Education*, Vol. 58, No. 3, July, pp. 191–200.

Viscusi, W.K. (1980), "A Theory of Job Shopping: A Bayesian Perspective", *Quarterly Journal of Economics*, May, pp. 609–614.

Walsh, B.M. (1984), *Does Ireland have a Special Problem of Youth Unemployment?* Centre for Economic Research, Policy Paper 10, Dublin: UCD Department of Political Economy.

Waitzman, N.J. and K.R. Smith (1994), "Procedure for Allocating Workers by Occupational Segment", Appendix to "The Effects of Occupational Class Transitions on Hypertension: Racial Disparities in a Cohort of Working-Aged Men", *American Journal of Public Health*, Vol. 84, Pt. 6, pp. 945–50.

Whelan, C.T. and B.J. Whelan (1984), *Social Mobility in the Republic of Ireland: A Comparative Perspective*, ESRI General Research Series No. 116, Dublin: The Economic and Social Research Institute.

Wielers, R. and A. Glebeek (1995), "Graduates and the Labour Market in the Netherlands: Three Hypotheses and Some Data", *European Journal of Education*, Vol. 30, No. 1, pp. 11–30.

Wilensky, H. and A. Lawrence (1979), "Job Assignment in Modern Societies: A Re-examination of the Ascription-Achievement Hypothesis" in A. Harvey (ed.), *Societal Growth: Processes and Implications*, New York: Free Press.